EDMONDS

Microwave Cookery Book

presented by the marketers of
Edmonds Sure to Rise Baking Powder
Edmonds Custard Powder, *Edmonds* Cake Mixes
Edmonds Pancake Mix, *Edmonds* Pikelet Mix
Edmonds Coat 'n' Cook, *Edmonds* Rice Risotto
Fielders Cornflour, *Champion* Flour, *Flemings* Rolled Oats
DYC Vinegar and Sauces, *DYC* Yeast
White Wings Cheesecake Mix, *White Wings* Sponge Pudding
Ready Recipe Scalloped Potatoes and Pasta Meals

Published for
BLUEBIRD FOODS LTD
Auckland, New Zealand

• INTRODUCTION TO EDMONDS MICROWAVE COOKBOOK

Microwave cookery requires a whole new approach. Everything you have learnt as a conventional cook needs to be put to one side and a new feel for cookery needs to be developed.

Microwave cooking times vary depending on the temperature of the food when it goes into the oven, whether the oven has been used to cook a number of foods in succession, the material of the cooking vessel and sometimes even the time of day.

Cooking times in this book are for a 700-watt microwave oven.

All cooking times are a guide only, NOT an absolute rule.

It is better to remember to choose the lowest time given in a microwave recipe as it is simple to add to the cooking time. There is no turning back if you overcook a food and in the microwave it happens so quickly.

These recipes were tested in a 700-watt oven.

To modify recipes for different wattage ovens, the following serves as a guide:-

650-watt add 5 seconds per minute
600-watt add 8 seconds per minute
500-watt add 20 seconds per minute

The words used to describe different power levels varies depending on the oven brand. This is why for all power levels other than High power, we have used the percentage power. Look in your oven manual and you will find an explanation of what each power level is called for your oven.

When trying a new recipe, slightly undercook the food then add extra time if necessary.

Turning food during cooking ensures it cooks evenly. This is only necessary if your microwave tends to cook unevenly.

• WEIGHTS AND MEASURES

All recipes in this book use standard metric measuring cups and measuring spoons. All measurements are taken as level.

1 cup	= 250 ml
1 tablespoon	= 15 ml
1 teaspoon	= 5 ml

Standard metric measures are inexpensive and are available at specialty plastic shops and hardware stores.

• METRIC WEIGHTS AND MEASURES EQUIVALENTS

• FLOUR

4 cups	= 500 grams
1 cup	= 125 grams
2 tablespoons	= 15 grams
2 teaspoons	= 5 grams

• BUTTER

2 cups	= 500 grams
1 cup	= 250 grams
1 tablespoon	= 15 grams
1 teaspoon	= 5 grams

• SUGAR

2 cups	= 500 grams
1 cup	= 250 grams
1 tablespoon	= 15 grams
1 teaspoon	= 5 grams

CONTENTS

MICROWAVE COOKING TIMES

Microwave cooking times may vary with the power of your oven. It is better to choose the shortest times given in a microwave recipe to avoid overcooking.

The recipes in this book were tested in a 700-watt oven. To modify recipes to match your microwave this table should help:
>   650-watt microwave, add 5 seconds per minute
>   600-watt microwave, add 8 seconds per minute
>   500-watt microwave, add 20 seconds per minute

Further helpful hints are contained in the Introduction.

• AFGOAT SLICE

200 g soft butter	1 teaspoon *Edmonds* baking powder
½ cup brown sugar	½ cup *Flemings* wholegrain oats
1 cup flour	½ cup chopped nuts
2 tablespoons cocoa	About ½ cup walnut halves

Cream butter and sugar until soft. Sift flour, cocoa and baking powder together. Add to creamed mixture along with wholegrain oats. Stir to combine. Press mixture into a 18cm x 22cm glass microwave slice dish. Elevate, then microwave on High power (100%) for 3 to 5 minutes. Allow to cool in tray then ice with chocolate icing. Decorate with walnut halves and cut into squares.

ICING:

2 tablespoons water	2 teaspoons butter
1 tablespoon cocoa	1 ½ cups icing sugar

In a glass-measuring jug mix the water and cocoa together until smooth. Add the butter. Microwave on High power for 1 minute or until cocoa goes dark and butter melted. Sift icing sugar and mix into cocoa mixture. Beat until smooth.

• AMERICAN YEAST COFFEE CAKE

¼ cup sugar	1 ½ teaspoons DYC dried yeast
½ teaspoon salt	2 cups flour
50 g butter	2 teaspoons mixed spice
¾ cup water	1 egg

In a large microwave jug put sugar, salt, butter and water. Microwave on High power (100%) for 40 seconds or until the liquid is just blood heat. Stir. Sprinkle yeast on top and leave in a warm place until frothy. Sift flour and mixed spice. Beat half the flour into the yeast mixture. Lightly beat the egg and add. Then beat in the remaining flour. The dough is fairly sticky. Spread into a 22cm loose bottom shallow microwave cake pan, using floured hands if necessary. Microwave on 30% power for 1 minute, leave for 10 minutes. Repeat until dough has doubled in size. Sprinkle with topping mixture. Elevate and cook on High for 3 minutes. Allow to cool then drizzle coffee icing on top.
Serves 8 to 10.

TOPPING:

25 g butter	2 tablespoons flour
¼ cup brown sugar	½ cup chopped walnuts

Put the butter and sugar in a microwave bowl. Microwave on High power (100%) for 30 seconds or until melted. Stir in the flour and nuts until mixture is crumbly.

ICING:

½ teaspoon instant coffee	½ teaspoon butter
2 teaspoons hot water	½ cup icing sugar

Mix together the coffee, hot water and butter. Gradually beat in the icing sugar until a soft icing is formed.

NOTE: This yeast cake should be served the day it is made.

• AMERICAN CHOCOLATE BROWNIES

150 g butter	1 cup flour
1 cup sugar	½ teaspoon *Edmonds* baking powder
2 eggs	½ teaspoon salt
2 tablespoons water	½ cup *Bournville* cocoa
1 teaspoon vanilla	½ cup walnuts, chopped

Melt butter on High power (100%) for 1½-2 minutes. Add sugar and mix well. Cool slightly then whisk in eggs, water and vanilla. Add flour, baking powder, salt and cocoa and mix until smooth. Stir in nuts. Pour into square baking dish which has been lined with baking paper. Shield corners with aluminium foil. Elevate and microwave on 50% power 10-11 minutes, removing foil after half cooking time. Cool in dish, sift with icing sugar and cut into squares.

• APPLE SPICE CAKE

3 cooking apples	½ cup oil
½ cup sultanas	1½ cups flour
¼ teaspoon ground cloves	1 teaspoon baking soda
2 tablespoons water	1 teaspoon mixed spice
2 eggs	½ cup chopped walnuts
¾ cup brown sugar	Icing sugar

Peel, core and finely chop apples. Stir in sultanas, cloves and water and cook on High power (100%) for 4 minutes. Cool slightly. Beat eggs and add to apples with sugar and oil. Sift together flour, baking soda and mixed spice and stir into apple mixture with chopped nuts. Grease and line the base of a medium-sized microwave ring mould. Turn mixture into prepared mould and smooth top. Elevate and cook on 70% power for about 8 to 9 minutes or until cooked through when tested with a skewer. Leave cake in container for 5 minutes before turning out. Cool and dust top with icing sugar. Serve with whipped cream if wished.

• APPLE WALNUT CAKE

1½ cups flour	½ teaspoon vanilla essence
2 teaspoons *Edmonds* baking powder	¼ cup milk
¼ teaspoon salt	3 large cooking apples
25 g butter	25 g butter
2 tablespoons brown sugar	½ cup brown sugar
½ cup chopped walnuts	2 teaspoons mixed spice
1 egg	

Sift flour, baking powder and salt together into a mixing bowl. Cut through the first measure of butter until crumb-like. Add first measure of sugar and walnuts. Lightly beat egg, vanilla and milk together. Stir into dry ingredients to form a smooth dough. Knead lightly until smooth. Use to line a 24cm round shallow microwave dish. Peel, quarter, core and finely slice apples. Arrange apple slices on top of dough. Put second measure of butter in a bowl. Microwave on High power (100%) for 1 minute or until melted. Brush melted butter over sliced apples. Combine second measure of sugar and mixed spice. Sprinkle over apples. Microwave on High for 6 to 7 minutes. Serve warm if wished.

• APRICOT AND DATE BARS

BASE:

1 cup flour	½ cup brown sugar
1 teaspoon *Edmonds* baking powder	100 g butter
1 cup *Flemings* rolled oats	

Sift flour and baking powder into the bowl of a food processor. Add rolled oats and sugar. Pulse to combine. Roughly chop the butter. Add to the processor and process until a crumbly mixture is formed. Reserve one cup of oat mixture. Press remaining mixture into a 18cm x 22cm glass microwave slice dish. Spread filling over base. Sprinkle reserved oat mixture on top. Elevate and microwave on High power (100%) for 5 minutes or until mixture looks cooked from underside. When cold cut into fingers.

FILLING:

1 cup chopped dried apricots	¼ cup sugar
1 cup chopped pitted dates	1 tablespoon lemon juice
½ cup water	

Put the apricots, dates, water, sugar and lemon juice into a one-litre glass microwave jug. Microwave on 50% power for 5 minutes.

• APRICOT COCONUT SLICE

30 g butter	½ cup castor sugar
½ cup sugar	1 egg
1 egg	1 cup coconut
1 cup flour	Few drops almond essence
1 teaspoon *Edmonds* baking powder	Extra coconut
Apricot jam	

Microwave butter and sugar on High power for 1 minute or until melted. Beat in egg until thick. Add flour and baking powder and mix to a stiff dough. Spread with apricot jam. Whisk second egg and sugar until thick, stir in coconut and almond essence and spread over jam. Sprinkle with extra coconut. Elevate and microwave on 75% power for about 9 minutes. Leave in dish and cut into bars while still warm.

• APRICOT MUESLI BARS

175 g butter	½ cup wheatgerm
¼ cup honey	1 cup puffed rice cereal
¼ cup golden syrup	2 cups *Flemings* rolled oats
½ cup flour	½ cup toasted coconut
¼ cup sugar	½ cup chopped, dried apricots
2 tablespoons sunflower kernels	

Put the butter, honey and golden syrup into a two-litre glass microwave measuring jug. Microwave on High power (100%) for 1 minute or until butter has melted. Put the flour, sugar, sunflower kernels, wheatgerm, rice cereal, rolled oats, coconut and apricots into a large mixing bowl. Mix to combine. Pour the melted ingredients into the bowl. Mix to thoroughly combine. Press mixture evenly into a 22cm x 30cm glass microwave slice dish. Elevate and microwave on High for 4 ½ minutes. Leave to stand 2 minutes. Cut into bars while warm. Allow to go cold before transferring to an airtight container.

• APRICOT SLICE

125 g butter
½ cup brown sugar
½ can sweetened condensed milk

1 cup chopped dried apricots
2¾ cups wine biscuit crumbs
¼ cup coconut

Put the butter, sugar and condensed milk into a glass microwave jug. Microwave on High power (100%) for 2 minutes or until butter melts. Do not allow mixture to boil. Stir after 1 minute. Add apricots and biscuit crumbs. Mix thoroughly. Press into a greased 20cm x 30cm sponge roll tin. Sprinkle with coconut. Refrigerate until set. To serve cut into squares.

• BANANA CAKE

125 g butter
1 cup castor sugar
1 teaspoon vanilla essence
3 ripe bananas
2 eggs
1 teaspoon baking soda

¼ cup warm milk
2 cups flour
2 teaspoons *Edmonds* baking
   powder
Icing sugar

Cream butter, sugar and vanilla together until soft. Peel and mash the bananas. Lightly beat the eggs. Combine banana and eggs. Add banana mixture to the creamed mixture. Dissolve the soda in milk. Add to banana mixture. Sift flour and baking powder together. Fold into banana mixture, mixing well. Lightly grease a 20cm microwave ring mould. Pour batter into prepared pan. Cover with a paper towel. Cook elevated on High power (100%) for 7 to 8 minutes or until cake looks just set on top. Allow to cool slightly before turning onto a cooling rack. When cool dust with icing sugar.

• BRAN MUFFINS

1 cup bran
1 cup *Flemings* oatbran
¼ cup brown sugar
1 cup milk
¼ cup treacle
1¼ cups flour
1 teaspoon *Edmonds* baking powder

1 teaspoon baking soda
½ teaspoon salt
½ cup raisins
½ cup oil
1 egg

In a mixing bowl combine bran, oatbran and sugar. Add milk and treacle, mix to combine. Sift flour, baking powder, baking soda and salt together. Stir raisins, oil and egg into bran mixture. Fold sifted ingredients into bran mixture until just moist. Spoon mixture into two layer muffin paper cases. Set into a microwave muffin pan. Microwave first five muffins on High power (100%) for about 2 minutes or until just set. Leave to stand 5 minutes. Repeat with remaining mixture.
Makes 10.

Use the containers stated in recipes as much as possible especially with baking.

BAKING

• CARROT CAKE

1 cup wholemeal flour	2 cups grated carrots
2 teaspoons *Edmonds* baking powder	½ cup oil
2 teaspoons mixed spice	2 eggs
¾ cup brown sugar	¼ cup chopped walnuts

Sift flour, baking powder and mixed spice into a mixing bowl. Add sugar, mix to combine. Beat carrots, oil and eggs together. Pour into mixing bowl, mix with a fork to just combine. Pour batter into a lined 20cm microwave ring mould. Cover and elevate. Cook on 70% power for 8 minutes. Stand for 5 minutes before turning onto a cooling rack. When cold ice with cream cheese icing. Sprinkle with walnuts.

ICING:

75 g butter	1 teaspoon vanilla essence
150 g pot cream cheese	2 cups icing sugar

Beat butter, cream cheese and vanilla together until soft. Sift icing sugar. Gradually beat icing sugar into cream mixture.

• CHERRY AND COCONUT CAKE

125 g butter	½ cup coconut
½ teaspoon vanilla essence	About ¼ cup milk
½ cup castor sugar	½ cup chopped cherries
2 eggs	Icing sugar
1½ cups flour	
2 teaspoons *Edmonds* baking powder	

Cream butter, vanilla and sugar until pale and soft. Beat in eggs one at a time. Sift flour and baking powder together. Fold sifted ingredients into creamed mixture. Stir in the coconut and sufficient milk to make a soft batter. Lightly grease and line a 20cm microwave ring mould. Sprinkle cherries over the base of mould. Pour batter on top. Elevate and microwave on High power (100%) for about 6 minutes or until just set. Leave to stand 10 minutes before turning on to a cooling rack. Dust with icing sugar when cold.

• CHOC-CHIP SLICE

100 g butter	2 tablespoons cocoa
2 eggs	1 teaspoon *Edmonds* baking powder
1 cup sugar	¾ cup chocolate chips
1 teaspoon vanilla essence	Icing sugar
1 cup flour	

Put butter in a one-litre glass microwave measuring jug. Cover. Microwave on High power (100%) for 1 minute or until butter has melted. Stir in the eggs, sugar and vanilla. Beat well with a wooden spoon. Sift flour, cocoa and baking powder together. Fold into egg mixture with chocolate chips. Do not overmix. Spoon batter into a lined 18cm x 22cm glass slice dish. Elevate and microwave on High for 5 to 7 minutes or until centre is just dry. Do not overcook. Leave in dish until cold. When cold dust with icing sugar and cut into squares.

• CHOCO-COFFEE CRUNCH

175 g butter
1 cup flour
1 teaspoon *Edmonds* baking powder
¼ cup cocoa

1 cup brown sugar
1 cup coconut
2 cups *Flemings* rolled oats

Put the butter in a bowl. Cover. Microwave on High power (100%) for 1½ minutes or until melted. Sift the flour, baking powder and cocoa into a mixing bowl. Add the sugar, coconut and oats. Mix well to combine. This is a dry mixture. Press into a 22cm x 30cm glass microwave slice dish. Elevate and microwave on High for 6 minutes or until centre looks dry from underside. Allow to cool before icing. When cold cut into squares.

ICING:

25 g butter
2 teaspoons instant coffee

2 tablespoons milk
2½ cups icing sugar

In a glass microwave jug put the butter, coffee and milk. Microwave on High power for 1 minute or until butter has melted. Stir to combine. Sift icing sugar and mix into melted ingredients to form a spreadable icing, adding more icing sugar if necessary.

• CHOCOLATE B.C. CRUNCH

100 g butter
1 tablespoon golden syrup
1 cup flour
1 teaspoon *Edmonds* baking powder
2 tablespoons cocoa

½ cup coconut
½ cup brown sugar
½ cup crushed wholewheat malted
   breakfast cereal biscuits
Icing sugar

Melt butter with golden syrup on High power (100%) for about 45 seconds. Sift together flour, baking powder and cocoa. Add to melted butter with coconut, brown sugar and crushed cereal biscuits. Mix well. Press into a glass microwave 18cm x 22cm slice dish. Smooth top. Cook on 70% power for 8 minutes. Mark out into squares while still warm. Sprinkle with icing sugar and cut into squares.

• CHOCOLATE CAKE

50 g butter
2 teaspoons golden syrup
½ cup sugar
1 egg
1 cup flour
2 tablespoons cocoa

½ teaspoon *Edmonds* baking
   powder
¾ teaspoon baking soda
¾ cup milk
1 teaspoon vanilla essence

Melt butter and golden syrup together on High power (100%) for 45 seconds. Mix in sugar then egg. Add flour, cocoa, baking powder, soda dissolved in milk and vanilla. Mix with a spoon, pressing out lumps. Pour into a 20cm ring mould, cover with a sheet of waxed paper and microwave on High power (100%) for about 4 minutes. Cool on a rack. Ice with chocolate icing.

If food is cooking unevenly, give a quarter turn during cooking.

BAKING

• CHOCOLATE CAKE

100 g butter	½ teaspoon baking soda
1 cup sugar	1¼ cups flour
2 tablespoons cocoa	1 teaspoon *Edmonds* baking powder
½ cup strong black coffee	1 egg

Put butter, sugar, cocoa, coffee and soda into a two-litre glass microwave jug. Microwave on High power (100%) for 3 minutes or until butter has melted. Stir to combine. Stand for 3 minutes. Sift flour and baking powder together. Add to the melted ingredients. Add the egg. Beat mixture until a smooth batter is formed. Pour batter into a 20cm microwave ring mould. Elevate and microwave on High for 4½ minutes, or until surface springs back when touched. Place an inverted plate on top of the mould for 2 minutes, then remove plate and allow cake to stand uncovered for 5 minutes. Unmould onto a cake rack. Ice when cold.

• LARGE MOIST CHOCOLATE CAKE

2 eggs	1½ cups flour
1 cup brown sugar	¼ cup cocoa
1 cup milk	1 teaspoon *Edmonds* baking powder
1 cup oil	1 teaspoon baking soda
¼ cup treacle	

Beat eggs, brown sugar, milk, oil and treacle together. Sift together flour, cocoa, baking powder and baking soda. Beat into egg mixture to form a smooth batter. Line the base of a large microwave ring mould with baking or grease-proof paper. Pour in cake mixture. Elevate and cook on 70% power for 12 minutes. Leave in container for 5 minutes on wooden board before turning out. Cool, then ice with chocolate icing or fill with whipped cream if wished.

• CHOC CARAMEL SLICE

150 g butter	1 tablespoon golden syrup
¾ cup brown sugar	400 g can sweetened condensed
2 cups flour	milk
1 teaspoon *Edmonds* baking powder	200 g cooking chocolate
50 g butter	

Cream first measure of butter and sugar until light and fluffy. Sift flour and baking powder and add to the creamed mixture. Mix well. Press mixture into a 22cm x 30cm glass microwave slice dish. Elevate and microwave on High power (100%) for 5½ minutes or until mixture looks dry in the centre from the underside of the dish. Set aside. Combine the second measure of butter, golden syrup and condensed milk in a two-litre glass microwave measuring jug. Cook on High for 3½ minutes or until thicker and starting to change colour. Stir twice during cooking. Spread the caramel over the base. Elevate and microwave on High for 2½ minutes or until caramel bubbles. Allow to cool slightly then spread with melted chocolate. Refrigerate until chocolate has set. Cut into fingers.

To Melt Chocolate:

Break chocolate into a glass bowl. Microwave on High power for about 2 minutes or until melted when stirred.

Chocolate melted in the microwave holds its shape until mixed.

• CHOCOLATE CRACKLES

25 g butter
100 g cooking chocolate
2 cups marshmallows

½ cup chopped unsalted roasted peanuts
3 cups puffed rice breakfast cereal

Put the butter in a one-litre glass microwave measuring jug. Cover. Microwave on High power (100%) for 1 minute. Break the chocolate and mix into the butter. Stir. Add the marshmallows. Microwave on 50% power for about 40 seconds or until melted. Stir in the peanuts and puffed rice cereal. Drop spoonsful of mixture into paper patty pans. Refrigerate until set.

• CHOCOLATE CUP CAKES

50 g butter
50 g brown sugar
1 egg, beaten
75 g self-raising flour

3 tablespoons *Bournville* cocoa
Pinch salt
120 ml milk

Microwave butter and sugar on full power for 10-20 seconds. Whisk until creamy. Add egg and whisk well. Mix in flour, cocoa and salt, alternately with milk. Mix until smooth. Place in microwave muffin cases in muffin tray. Half fill each case, elevate and microwave on High power (100%) for 2 minutes (6 cup cakes) or 1 minute 40 seconds (5 cup cakes). Remove cases from muffin trays immediately and cool on cake rack.

• CHOCOLATE ROUGH

120 g butter
⅓ cup castor sugar
½ cup coconut

1 cup self-raising flour
2 teaspoons *Bournville* cocoa
Pinch of salt

Melt butter on High power (100%) for 1 minute. Stir in remaining ingredients. Press into square baking dish and microwave on 75% power for about 5½ minutes or until just firm. Cool slightly. Spread with the following topping while still warm and cut into slices when cold.

TOPPING:

30 g butter
3 tablespoons condensed milk
1 tablespoon *Bournville* cocoa

1 cup icing sugar
1 cup coconut
1 teaspoon vanilla

Melt butter on High power (100%) for 40-60 seconds. Stir in remaining ingredients and mix well.

The denser the texture of a food the longer the cooking process carries on after food is taken from the oven.

Don't be afraid to open the microwave oven door and check cooking.   11

• CHOCOLATE WALNUT SLICE

1 ¼ cups flour	½ cup walnuts
1 teaspoon *Edmonds* baking powder	125 g butter
¼ cup cocoa	2 tablespoons chopped walnuts
½ cup brown sugar	

Put the flour, baking powder, cocoa and sugar into the bowl of a food processor. Pulse to combine. Add the first measure of walnuts. Put the butter in a glass microwave measuring jug. Cover. Microwave on High (100%) for 1 minute, or until melted. With motor running, pour the melted butter down the feed tube. Process until just combined. Press into a 18cm x 22cm glass microwave slice dish. Elevate and microwave on High for 5 minutes or until the centre looks cooked from underside. Ice the slice while still warm. Sprinkle with chopped walnuts.

ICING:

50 g butter	1 tablespoon milk
2 teaspoons water	About 1 ½ cups icing sugar
1 tablespoon cocoa	

Put the butter, water, cocoa and milk into a glass microwave measuring jug. Microwave on High power for about 1 ½ minutes or until butter has melted and mixture thickens. Add the icing sugar, beating to combine. If necessary more water can be added to give a spreadable icing.

• CHRISTMAS CAKE

1 ½ kg mixed fruit	2 teaspoons mixed spice
1 cup chopped crystallised ginger	1 teaspoon ground cinnamon
¼ cup chopped glacé cherries	½ teaspoon ground nutmeg
1 ½ cups sliced almonds	1 ½ teaspoons grated lemon rind
250 g butter	3 tablespoons treacle
1 ¼ cups brown sugar	6 tablespoons brandy
1 to 2 tablespoons gravy browning	2 to 3 tablespoons extra brandy
6 eggs	for sprinkling
2 cups flour	

Place the mixed fruit, ginger, cherries and almonds in a bowl. In a large bowl, cream the butter and sugar. Add the gravy browning. Separate the eggs and add the yolks to the creamed mixture. Beat until well mixed. Stir in half the flour. Gradually mix in the fruit. Beat the egg whites until soft peaks form. Fold into the cake mixture. Add the remaining flour, mixed spice, cinnamon, nutmeg, lemon rind, treacle and brandy. Spread the mixture into a large 28cm microwave dish. Elevate and microwave on 50% power for 1 hour 10 minutes. Test and cook a further 10 minutes on 50% if required. Stand cake in dish for 2 hours. Remove from dish and when cool sprinkle with extra brandy. Store in a cool, dark place wrapped in greaseproof paper and foil.

Always use microwave-safe plastic wrap for microwave cooking. This is marked on the box or wrapper.

• COBERG CAKES

50 g butter
½ cup brown sugar
½ cup golden syrup
1 cup milk
2 teaspoons ground ginger

1 teaspoon baking soda
1½ cups flour
½ teaspoon salt
12 roasted almonds

Put the butter, sugar, syrup, milk and ginger into a two-litre glass microwave measuring jug. Microwave on High power (100%) for about 2 minutes or until butter has melted. Stir well, add soda and allow to stand 2 minutes. Sift flour and salt together. Beat sifted ingredients into melted mixture. Put paper patty cases into microwave patty pans. Two-thirds fill patty pans with batter. Elevate and microwave on High for 30 seconds. Place an almond on top of each cake. Cook for a further 40 seconds on 90% power or until just firm to touch. Allow to cool. Repeat with remaining mixture until all batter is used.

• COCONUT ROUGH SLICE

BASE:

125 g butter
1 cup flour
1 teaspoon *Edmonds* baking powder

1 tablespoon cocoa
¼ cup sugar
½ cup *Flemings* oat bran

Put butter in a two-litre glass microwave measuring jug. Cover. Microwave on High power (100%) for 1 minute or until melted. Sift the flour, baking powder and cocoa together. Add sifted ingredients to the jug along with the sugar and oat bran. Mix to combine. Press into a 18cm x 22cm glass microwave slice dish. Elevate and microwave on High for 4 to 4½ minutes or until the centre looks cooked from the underside of the dish. Cool then ice. Cut into triangles when cold.

ICING:

1 teaspoon butter
½ cup sweetened condensed milk
¾ cup coconut

1 cup icing sugar
2 tablespoons cocoa
½ teaspoon vanilla essence

In a bowl combine butter, sweetened condensed milk and coconut. Sift icing sugar and cocoa together. Add sifted ingredients and vanilla to coconut mixture. Mix thoroughly to combine to make a soft spreadable icing. If necessary a small amount of hot water can be added.

• COFFEE MERINGUES

1 egg white
1 teaspoon instant coffee
1 teaspoon water

About 2 cups icing sugar
Whipped cream

Beat egg white until very stiff. Combine coffee and water. Stir into egg white. Sift icing sugar and add to egg white until a stiff pliable dough is formed. Roll dough into balls about the size of a walnut. Place around the edge of a lined large microwave plate. Microwave on High power (100%) for 1 minute 20 seconds. Remove from microwave and allow meringues to cool and harden. When cold sandwich together with whipped cream or coffee flavoured cream. Makes 9.

BAKING

• COFFEE-BREAK CAKE

2 cups flour
3 teaspoons *Edmonds* baking powder
¼ teaspoon salt
¼ cup sugar

1 egg
¼ cup oil
¾ cup milk

Sift flour, baking powder and salt. Add sugar then make a well and add the egg, oil and milk. Mix to a soft dough. Line the bottom of a 20cm casserole dish with greaseproof paper and spread mixture evenly in dish. Cover with a sheet of waxed paper and microwave on High power (100%) for 5-7 minutes. Ice when cool.

ICING:

Microwave 1 tablespoon butter and 1 tablespoon milk on High (100%) for 30 seconds then mix in 2 tablespoons brown sugar, 1 teaspoon cinnamon and ½ cup icing sugar.

• COFFEE HAZELNUT RING WITH GLACÉ ICING

120 g butter
120 g castor sugar
2 eggs
70 g hazelnuts

¼ cup milk
120 g flour
1 teaspoon *Edmonds* baking powder

Place butter and sugar in large jug or mixing bowl. Microwave on High power (100%) for 20-30 seconds or until butter softens. Whisk together until creamed. Add eggs, one at a time, adding a tablespoon of flour with each. Mix well. Stir in finely chopped hazelnuts and milk. Fold in rest of flour and baking powder with a metal spoon. Spoon mixture into a medium sized ring mould, elevate, cover with a sheet of paper towel and microwave on 75% power for about 7½ minutes, removing paper towel after 6 minutes. Stand 2 minutes before turning out. Cover cake while cooling with paper towels or teatowel and ice with Coffee Glacé Icing when cold.

ICING:

240 g icing sugar
2 teaspoons instant coffee powder
2 tablespoons hot water

Dissolve coffee powder in water. Gradually add to sifted icing sugar. Stir briskly till smooth then pour over cake.

• CUP CAKES

125 g butter
½ cup castor sugar
1 teaspoon vanilla essence
2 eggs

1 cup flour
1 teaspoon *Edmonds* baking powder
About ¼ cup milk

Cream butter, sugar and vanilla until pale and creamy. Lightly beat the eggs. Gradually add to creamed mixture, beating well after each addition. Sift flour and baking powder. Fold into creamed mixture. Add sufficient milk until a soft batter is formed. Double line a six-muffin pan tray with paper patty cups. Half fill each patty pan with batter. Elevate and microwave on 90% power for about 2 minutes or until surface is just set. Repeat with remaining batter. When cold ice and decorate as wished.
Makes 12.

• CREAM CHEESE SLICE

BASE:

150 g butter
½ cup brown sugar
1 egg
1 teaspoon grated lemon rind

1 ½ cups flour
1 teaspoon *Edmonds* baking powder
½ *Flemings* rolled oats
1 teaspoon mixed spice

Put the butter and sugar into the bowl of a food processor fitted with a metal blade. Process until creamy. Add egg and lemon rind, process for about 30 seconds or until blended. Sift flour and baking powder together. Sprinkle the sifted ingredients and oats over the creamed mixture. Pulse to combine. Press two-thirds of the mixture into a lightly greased 18cm x 22m glass microwave slice dish. Microwave on High power (100%) for 2 ½ minutes. Carefully spread the cream cheese filling over the base. Sprinkle the remaining third of cake mixture on top. Sprinkle with mixed spice. Elevate and microwave on High for 3 minutes. Reduce heat to 50% power for a further 3 minutes or until filling is cooked and set. Allow to cool in the tray. Cut into squares.

FILLING:

250 g pot cream cheese
1 egg
2 tablespoons brown sugar

1 teaspoon grated lemon rind
1 tablespoon lemon juice

Beat cream cheese until soft. Beat in the egg, sugar, lemon rind and juice until smooth.

• CURRANT BUNS

2 eggs
2 tablespoons brown sugar
2 tablespoons oil
1 cup flour

1 teaspoon mixed spice
2 teaspoons *Edmonds* baking powder
2 tablespoons currants
¼ cup milk

Beat eggs, sugar and oil until fluffy then mix in flour, baking powder, currants and milk with a spoon. Half fill muffin cups or paper patty pans and microwave 5 at a time on High power (100%) for about 1 minute 30 seconds. Cool on a rack. Ice with chocolate icing.

• CUSTARD KISSES

175 g butter
¾ cup icing sugar
1 teaspoon vanilla

1 ½ cups flour
½ cup *Edmonds* custard powder
1 teaspoon *Edmonds* baking powder

Place butter in mixing bowl and microwave on High power (100%) for 10-20 seconds, until soft but not melted. Beat in the remaining ingredients. Form mixture into a cylinder shape and chill in the freezer or fridge until very cold. Cut into 5mm thick slices. Press a halved cherry or walnut into each biscuit, or bake plain and sandwich together with the following icing. Line turntable with baking paper and place six biscuits around edge. Microwave on High for 1 ½ -2 minutes or until biscuits are just firm. Leave on the paper for a further minute then remove to a cake rack. They will crisp on standing.

ICING:

3 tablespoons softened butter
¾ cup icing sugar

1 tablespoon *Edmonds* custard powder
Water, if necessary to mix.

BAKING

• DATE AND NUT LOAF

¾ cup chopped walnuts
1 cup chopped dates
1 teaspoon baking soda
½ teaspoon salt
3 tablespoons butter

¾ cup boiling water
1 cup sugar
½ teaspoon vanilla
1½ cups flour
2 lightly beaten eggs

Place walnuts, dates, soda, salt and butter in large jug or bowl. Pour over boiling water and mix lightly. Stand for 20 minutes. Add sugar and vanilla and stir. Add flour and eggs and mix well. Pour into medium-sized ring mould, elevate, cover with a sheet of paper towel and microwave on 75% power for 8½-10 minutes. Stand 3 minutes and turn out. As soon as steam has disappeared, cover with a teatowel.

• ENGLISH MADELINES

125 g butter
½ cup castor sugar
2 eggs
1 teaspoon vanilla essence
1 cup flour

1 teaspoon *Edmonds* baking powder
About ¼ cup milk
About ½ cup jam
About ½ cup coconut
4 glacé cherries

Cream butter and sugar until light and fluffy. Lightly beat eggs. Gradually beat in eggs and vanilla, beating well after each addition. Sift flour and baking powder. Fold sifted ingredients into creamed mixture. Add sufficient milk to form a soft batter. Lightly grease four microwave pudding cups. Two-thirds fill each cup with batter. Elevate and microwave on 90% power for 2 minutes, or until just set. Leave for 2 minutes. Turn onto a cooling rack. Repeat with remaining batter. When sponge is cold, put the jam into a glass microwave measuring jug. Microwave on High for 1 to 2 minutes until heated and almost boiling. Brush each madeline with jam then roll in coconut. Top each one with half a glacé cherry.

NOTE: These are slightly more pudding-like than madelines cooked conventionally.

• FRUITY CARROT CAKE

1½ cups mixed fruit
1½ cups grated carrot
¾ cup water
¾ cup brown sugar
75 g butter

2 teaspoons cinnamon
1 teaspoon ground allspice
2 cups flour
1 teaspoon *Edmonds* baking powder
1 teaspoon baking soda

Put fruit, carrot, water, sugar, butter, cinnamon and allspice into a two-litre glass microwave measuring jug. Microwave on High power (100%) for 5 minutes, stirring every 2 minutes. Cover. Cook on 30% power for a further 10 minutes. Allow to cool. Sift flour, baking powder and soda. Fold sifted ingredients into cooled mixture. Pour batter into a 22cm microwave ring mould. Cover with a paper towel. Elevate and microwave on 90% power for 8 minutes or until just set. Allow to stand 10 minutes before turning out.

• FUDGE SLICE

125 g butter
3 tablespoons cocoa
½ cup water
1 cup sugar
1 cup flour
¼ teaspoon salt

1 teaspoon *Edmonds* baking powder
1 egg
¼ cup milk
½ teaspoon vanilla essence
¼ cup *Flemings* oat bran

ICING:

1 teaspoon grated orange rind
2 tablespoons orange juice

1 teaspoon butter
About 2 cups icing sugar

Put butter, cocoa and water in a two-litre glass microwave jug. Microwave on High power (100%) for 2 minutes or until butter is melted. Stir after 1 minute. Stir in the sugar. Allow to cool. Sift flour, salt and baking powder. Beat egg, milk and vanilla together. Fold sifted ingredients into jug along with oat bran. Add egg mixture, beating until smooth. Pour batter into a lightly greased 22cm x 30cm glass microwave slice dish. Microwave on 90% power for 9 minutes or until top is slightly moist in centre. Cool in dish. When cold ice with orange icing. Mark icing with a fork.

ICING:

Put orange rind, juice and butter in a microwave bowl. Cover and microwave on High power for 30 seconds or until butter has melted. Sift icing sugar. Add sufficient icing sugar to bowl and mix until a smooth spreadable icing is formed.

• GINGER CRUNCH

125 g butter
½ cup brown sugar
1½ cups flour

¾ teaspoon *Edmonds* baking powder
1 teaspoon ground ginger

ICING:

50g butter
1 tablespoon golden syrup
½ cup icing sugar

1 teaspoon ground ginger
¼ finely chopped crystallised ginger

Beat butter and sugar until soft. Sift flour, baking powder and ginger. Stir dry ingredients into creamed mixture, mixing well. Press into a 22cm x 30cm glass microwave slice dish. Elevate and microwave on High power (100%) for about 3½ minutes or until base looks cooked from underside. Allow to cool. When cold ice with ginger icing. Cut into squares when icing has set.

ICING:

Put butter and golden syrup into a glass jug. Cook on High power for 30 seconds or until butter has melted. Sift icing sugar and ginger. Add to melted ingredients. Stir well. Cook icing on High for a further 30 seconds. Fold in the crystallised ginger.

BAKING

• GINGERBREAD SLICE

50g butter
½ cup brown sugar
½ golden syrup
1 cup milk
2 teaspoons ground ginger

1 teaspoon mixed spice
1 teaspoon baking soda
1½ cups flour
½ teaspoon salt
Icing sugar

In a two-litre microwave jug put the butter, sugar, golden syrup, milk, ginger and mixed spice. Microwave on High power (100%) for about 2 minutes or until butter has melted, stirring after 1 minute. Stir again. Add the soda, mixing well, allow to stand for 2 minutes. Sift flour and salt together. Beat sifted ingredients into jug until a smooth batter is formed. Pour into a 22cm x 30cm glass microwave slice dish. Elevate and microwave on High for 4 to 5 minutes or until top surface looks dry. Allow to cool in dish. When cold dust with icing sugar.

• HAZELNUT SLICE

70 g packet hazelnuts
1 teaspoon oil
250 g packet wine biscuits

¼ cup brown sugar
125 g butter
½ can sweetened condensed milk

Put the hazelnuts and oil into a shallow glass microwave dish. Cook on High power (100%) for about 5 minutes or until roasted, allow to cool. Process in a blender or food processor until finely chopped. Crush the biscuits to fine crumbs. Add the brown sugar and chopped nuts to crumbs. Put the butter and sweetened condensed milk into a microwave glass jug. Microwave on High for 2 minutes, stirring after 1 minute. Add microwaved ingredients to the hazelnut mixture. Stir well to combine. Press mixture evenly into a 20cm x 30cm sponge roll tin. Refrigerate until firm. Cut into triangles and drizzle with melted chocolate if wished.

• HONEY GINGERBREAD LOAF

¼ cup honey
100 g butter
½ brown sugar
¾ cup milk
1 egg

1 teaspoon baking soda
2 cups flour
1 teaspoon mixed spice
1 teaspoon cinnamon
2 teaspoons ground ginger

Put the honey, butter, brown sugar and milk into a two-litre glass microwave measuring jug. Microwave on High power (100%) for about 3 minutes or until butter has melted, stirring after 1 minute. Allow to cool slightly. Beat in the egg and soda. Sift together the flour, mixed spice, cinnamon and ginger. Beat in the sifted ingredients. Pour into a lined 25cm x 10½cm x 7cm glass loaf dish. Cover with a paper towel. Elevate and microwave on High for 4 to 5 minutes or until just set. Allow to stand for 5 minutes. Pour topping over.

TOPPING:

2 tablespoons honey
¼ cup finely chopped crystallised ginger

Put the honey and ginger into a microwave bowl. Microwave on High for 1 minute.

Small amounts of food cook better than large amounts in the microwave.

• LEMON AND FRUIT SLICE

175 g butter
¾ cup brown sugar
1 egg
1 teaspoon lemon essence
1 cup mixed fruit

1 ½ cups flour
1 teaspoon *Edmonds* baking powder
1 teaspoon mixed spice
¼ cup coconut

ICING:

1 teaspoon grated lemon rind
2 tablespoons lemon juice

2 teaspoons butter
About 1 ½ cups icing sugar

Put butter in a glass microwave two-litre measuring jug. Cover and microwave on High power (100%) for 1 minute or until melted. Stir in the brown sugar, egg, essence and fruit. Sift flour, baking powder and mixed spice. Add to melted ingredients, mixing well. Spread mixture evenly into a lightly greased 22cm x 30cm glass microwave slice dish. Elevate and microwave on High for 5 to 6 minutes, or until just cooked in the centre. Allow to cool in the dish. When cold ice with lemon icing and sprinkle with coconut.

ICING:

Put the lemon rind and juice into a microwave bowl or jug. Microwave on High power for 1 minute. Stir in the butter then beat in icing sugar until a smooth, spreadable icing is formed.

• LEMON OATY SQUARES

100 g butter
¼ cup brown sugar
¼ cup castor sugar
2 cups *Flemings* rolled oats

¼ cup flour
½ cup coconut
½ cup chocolate chips

LEMON ICING:

25 g butter
1 tablespoon water
1 tablespoon lemon juice

1 teaspoon grated lemon rind
About 1 ½ cups icing sugar

Put the butter and sugars into a mixing bowl. Cover. Microwave on High power (100%) for 1 minute or until butter has melted. Stir to combine. Add rolled oats, flour, coconut and chocolate chips. Mix well. Press into a 18cm x 22cm glass microwave slice dish. Elevate and microwave on High for 3 minutes or until bubbling all over, taking care that the middle does not start to burn. Spread slice with lemon icing. Allow to cool before cutting into squares.

ICING:

Put the butter, water, lemon juice and rind into a one-litre glass microwave measuring jug. Microwave on High power for 2 minutes or until just boiling. Add the icing sugar beating well to form a soft, spreadable icing.

Every microwave oven is different. Treat cooking time given in a recipe as a guide NOT an absolute rule.

BAKING

• LEMON FINGERS

400 g can sweetened condensed milk	200 g packet malt biscuits
½ cup lemon juice	¼ cup brown sugar
1 teaspoon grated lemon rind	100 g butter

Beat together the condensed milk, lemon juice and rind until thick. In a separate bowl combine biscuit crumbs and sugar. Melt butter in microwave on High power (100%) for 1 minute. Add to crumb mixture, mixing thoroughly. Lightly grease a 22cm x 30cm glass microwave slice dish. Press two-thirds of biscuit mixture evenly into prepared dish. Spread lemon mixture evenly over the base. Sprinkle remaining crumb mixture on top. Gently pat down. Elevate and microwave on High for 6 minutes or until centre feels firm when pressed lightly with finger. Allow to cool in dish. When cold cut into fingers.

• MARMALADE CAKE

2 cups flour	1 teaspoon orange peel
2 teaspoons *Edmonds* baking powder	2 eggs
Pinch of salt	4 tablespoons milk
120 g butter	4 tablespoons orange marmalade
60 g castor sugar	

Place flour, baking powder and salt into food processor bowl, cut butter into cubes and process until the consistency of fine crumbs. (Alternatively, rub butter into flour, baking powder and salt.) Add sugar and orange peel. Mix to a soft batter with eggs beaten with milk and marmalade. Place in medium ring mould, elevate, cover with a sheet of paper towel and microwave on 75% power for about 7½ minutes, removing paper towel after 6 minutes. Stand 2 minutes before turning out. Cover cake while cooling with paper towels or teatowel. Note: This is a pale cake and can be iced with an orange butter icing.

• MARSHMALLOW SLICE

100 g butter
1 ½ cups biscuit crumbs

TOPPING:

190 g packet pink and white marshmallows	¼ cup coconut
½ cup cream	1 ½ tablespoons coconut

Put the butter into a one-litre glass microwave measuring jug. Cover and microwave on High power (100%) for 1 minute or until melted. Add the biscuit crumbs, mixing well to combine. Press into a 18cm x 22cm shallow tray. Refrigerate until firm. In a glass bowl combine the marshmallows and cream. Microwave on 50% power for 1 minute. Stir, then continue cooking for a further 30 seconds, checking every 10 seconds until marshmallows have melted. Stir in the first measure of coconut. Allow to cool slightly then pour on top of biscuit base. Sprinkle second measure of coconut on top. Refrigerate until set. Cut into squares.

Choose even-sized foods for easier more even cooking.

• MERINGUE SLICE

100 g butter
¼ cup brown sugar
1 ½ cups flour
1 teaspoon *Edmonds* baking powder

¼ cup strawberry jam
1 egg white
¾ cup icing sugar
½ cup coconut

Cream butter and sugar until pale. Sift flour and baking powder. Fold into creamed mixture, mixing well. Press into a 18cm x 22cm glass microwave slice dish. Elevate and microwave on High power (100%) for 2 ½ minutes. Allow to stand 5 minutes. Spread base with jam. In a separate bowl beat egg white until stiff. Sift icing sugar and fold into the egg white with the coconut. Carefully spread meringue over the jam. Elevate and microwave on High for 2 to 3 minutes or until the whole surface has risen. This will go down on cooling. Cut when cold.

• MIDDLE EASTERN SQUARES

1 cup semolina
1 ¼ cups flour
1 teaspoon *Edmonds* baking powder
½ cup sugar
125 g butter
½ teaspoon vanilla essence

1 ½ cups chopped dates
6 tablespoons water
2 tablespoons honey or corn syrup
1 tablespoon lemon juice
½ teaspoon cinnamon
1 cup chopped walnuts

In a bowl combine semolina, flour, baking powder and sugar. Mix well. Melt butter and add, with vanilla, to dry ingredients. Mix till well combined. Place chopped dates and water in bowl and microwave, uncovered, on High power (100%) for 3 minutes. Add honey, lemon juice, cinnamon and nuts. Stir well. Place half semolina mixture in 20cm square dish. Press down well. Spread date mixture evenly on top. Sprinkle remaining semolina mixture over dates, elevate and microwave, uncovered, on 75% power for 11 minutes. Leave to cool in dish and cut into squares.

• MUESLI BARS

75 g butter
½ cup brown sugar
¼ cup honey
1 ½ cups *Flemings* wholegrain red oats
½ cup coconut
½ cup sultanas

½ cup sliced almonds
¼ cup sesame seeds
½ cup wholemeal flour
½ teaspoon *Edmonds* baking powder

Heat together butter, brown sugar and honey on High power (100%) for 2 to 3 minutes. Mix well then add oats, coconut, sultanas, sliced almonds and sesame seeds. Sift together wholemeal flour and baking powder and stir into mixture to form a stiff dough. Press into a glass microwave 18cm x 22cm slice dish. Smooth top. Cook on 70% power for 10 minutes. Mark out into squares while still warm. Cut into squares and lift out of container when cold.

BAKING

• OAT CAKE WITH NUT TOPPING

½ cup *Flemings* rolled oats
1 ¼ cups water
50 g butter
2 eggs
½ teaspoon microwave browning liquid
1 cup flour

1 teaspoon baking soda
½ teaspoon *Edmonds* baking powder
½ teaspoon cinnamon
½ teaspoon ground nutmeg
1 cup brown sugar

TOPPING:

¼ cup cream cheese
¼ cup coarsely chopped nuts

½ cup coconut
¼ cup brown sugar

Mix together rolled oats and water and cook on High power (100%) for 4 minutes. Melt butter on High for about 30 seconds. Beat eggs. Add butter, eggs and browning liquid into cooked oats. Sift together flour, baking soda, baking powder, cinnamon and nutmeg. Stir into oat mixture with brown sugar. Lightly grease and line the base of a medium-sized microwave ring mould with a flat bottom (or use a round dish with a glass inside). Turn mixture into prepared container and smooth top. Elevate and cook on 70% power or until just cooked. The top surface will still look slightly damp. Leave 10 minutes before turning out on a plate. Spread topping over cake and brown gently under grill.

TOPPING:

Warm cream cheese on High power (100%) for 30 seconds. Stir in nuts, coconut and brown sugar.

• ORANGE MUESLI SLICE

200 g butter
¾ cup brown sugar
2 tablespoons golden syrup
3 ½ cups *Flemings* rolled oats

½ cup sultanas
2 teaspoons grated orange rind
1 teaspoon mixed spice

ICING:

2 teaspoons butter
2 tablespoons orange juice

1 teaspoon grated orange rind
2 cups icing sugar

In a two-litre glass microwave measuring jug put the butter, sugar and golden syrup. Cover. Microwave on High power (100%) for 2 minutes or until butter has melted. Stir. Add oats, sultanas, orange rind and mixed spice. Mix thoroughly. Press into a 22cm x 30cm glass microwave slice dish. Elevate and microwave on High for 6 to 8 minutes or until dry on top. Allow to cool completely. Ice with orange icing. Cut into squares.

ICING:

Beat together butter, orange juice, rind and icing sugar until a smooth spreadable icing is formed.

Cakes should be removed from the microwave when they are just cooked on the surface.

• PEANUT BROWNIE

100 g butter
½ cup sugar
2 cups flour
2 teaspoons *Edmonds* baking powder

1 tab... ...coa
1 egg
½ cup roasted peanuts
Icing sugar

Put butter into a one cup glass microwave measuring jug. Cover. Microwave on High power (100%) for 1 minute or until melted. Put the sugar, flour, baking powder and cocoa into the bowl of a food processor. Pulse to combine. Beat butter and egg together. With motor running pour the butter mixture down the feed tube. Process until well mixed. Press mixture into a 22cm x 30cm glass microwave slice dish. Press chopped nuts on top. Microwave elevated on High for 4 minutes or until slice looks cooked from underside. Allow to cool in dish. When cold dust with icing sugar.

To Roast Nuts:

Put peanuts and half a teaspoon of oil into a glass pie plate. Microwave on High for 2 to 3 minutes or until roasted. Stir at least twice during cooking. Roughly chop the nuts before putting on the slice.

• PEANUT BROWNIES

125 g butter
1 cup sugar
1 egg
1½ cups flour
½ cup cornflour

¾ teaspoon *Edmonds* baking powder
1½ tablespoons *Bournville* cocoa
1 cup peanuts
¼ teaspoon salt

Place butter and sugar in a large bowl or jug and microwave on High power (100%) for 20-30 seconds. Whisk well and add egg, flour, cornflour, baking powder, salt, peanuts and cocoa. Form into balls, line turntable with baking paper and place 6 peanut brownies around edge. Microwave on High power (100%) for 2 minutes. Leave on turntable for 1 minute then remove to cake rack. Brownies will crisp as they cool.

• PEANUT BUTTER BAR

¼ cup crunchy peanut butter
½ cup brown sugar
50 g butter
1 egg

¼ teaspoon vanilla essence
½ cup flour
½ teaspoon baking soda
¼ cup *Flemings* rolled oats

Beat together the first measure of peanut butter, brown sugar and butter. Beat in egg and vanilla. Sift flour and baking soda into a bowl. Mix in the rolled oats. Add dry ingredients to peanut butter mixture, mixing well. Spread mixture into a 18cm x 22cm glass microwave slice dish. Elevate and microwave on High power (100%) for 3 to 5 minutes, or until base looks dry in centre from the underside, Allow to cool before spreading with topping. When topping has set cut into fingers. Store in an airtight container.

Topping:

¼ cup crunchy peanut butter
100 g cooking chocolate

Put peanut butter and chocolate into a bowl. Microwave on 70% power for 2 to 3 minutes, or until melted. Stir to combine.

BAKING

• PUMPKIN CAKE WITH CREAM CHEESE FROSTING

2 eggs
½ cup oil
1 cup sugar
250 g cooked mashed pumpkin
1 cup wholemeal flour
½ teaspoon baking soda

1 teaspoon cinnamon
¼ teaspoon ginger
¼ teaspoon ground cloves
¼ teaspoon nutmeg
1 teaspoon *Edmonds* baking powder
¼ teaspoon salt

Blend eggs, oil, sugar and pumpkin together in a large jug or bowl. Measure flour, baking soda, cinnamon, ginger, cloves, nutmeg, baking powder and salt into another bowl and mix together lightly with a fork. Stir into pumpkin mixture. Pour batter into small ring mould. Elevate, cover with a sheet of paper towel and microwave on High power (100%) for 5½ minutes, removing paper towel after 4 minutes. Let stand until almost cool then turn out and frost with cream cheese frosting.

• CREAM CHEESE FROSTING

90 g cream cheese
60 g butter
1 ½ teaspoons cream or milk

½ teaspoon vanilla
2 cups sifted icing sugar

Combine cream cheese and butter in medium mixing bowl or jug. Microwave on 20% power for 1 minute or until soft but not melted. Stir in cream and vanilla. Add icing sugar gradually until frosting reaches spreading consistency.

• QUEEN CAKES

ı cup flour
1 teaspoon mixed spice
1 teaspoon cinnamon
¼ cup sugar
1 teaspoon grated lemon rind
1 cup mixed fruit

25 g butter
1 cup milk
1 tablespoon DYC vinegar
1 teaspoon baking soda
Icing sugar

Sift flour, mixed spice and cinnamon into a mixing bowl. Stir in the sugar, lemon rind and mixed fruit. Make a well in the centre. Microwave the butter and milk on High power (100%) for 1 minute or until butter has melted. Add the vinegar and soda to the milk. Stir until soda has dissolved. Pour the liquid into the well. Stir to combine. Half fill lightly greased microwave patty pans with batter. Elevate and microwave on 70% power for about 1 minute 15 seconds or until just set. Leave to stand about 2 minutes before turning out. Repeat with remaining mixture. To serve invert and dust with icing sugar.
Makes about 12.

Read your oven manual to check power level descriptions.

Microwave baked cakes are generally best eaten on the day of cooking.

• SAVOURY MUFFINS

1 cup flour
½ teaspoon *Edmonds* baking powder
¼ teaspoon salt
1 cup grated cheese
¼ teaspoon mixed herbs
1 tablespoon finely chopped green
    pepper

1 tablespoon finely chopped parsley
1 egg
¼ cup milk
¼ cup water
1 teaspoon paprika

Sift the flour, baking powder and salt into a bowl. Stir in the cheese, herbs, pepper and parsley. Lightly beat the egg, milk and water together. Add to the cheese mixture. Stir to just moisten. Do not overmix. Spoon mixture into a greased microwave muffin tray. Sprinkle tops with paprika. Elevate and microwave on High power (100%) for about 3 minutes or until set and sponge-like on top. Stand 2 minutes. Serve hot.
Makes 6.

• SCONES

1½ cups self-raising flour
¼ teaspoon salt
30 g butter

1 egg
½ cup milk, approx.

Sift flour and salt and rub in butter till mixture resembles fine breadcrumbs. Beat egg lightly and add to dry ingredients with enough milk to give a soft dough. Turn onto floured surface and knead lightly. Pat out to approximately 20cm in diameter. Cut diagonally into eight equal pieces. Heat browning dish on High power (100%) for 6 minutes. Spread a little butter on dish. Place scones on browning dish in a circle, fairly close together and microwave on High power for 2 minutes. Turn and microwave a further 2 minutes. Serve immediately. Makes 8.

• SLICE AND BAKE WHOLE WHEAT CHOCOLATE CHIP BISCUITS

1½ cups packed brown sugar
1½ teaspoons baking soda
½ teaspoon salt
190 g butter or margarine
2 eggs

1½ teaspoons vanilla
2 cups plain flour
1½ cups wholemeal flour
1½ cups chocolate chips

In a large bowl mix brown sugar, baking soda, salt, butter, eggs and vanilla until light and fluffy. Stir in remaining ingredients. Divide dough into four equal parts. Shape each part into a roll approximately 15cm long (shaping is made easier by using plastic wrap). Wrap each roll in plastic wrap then in foil or plastic bag. Label and freeze no longer than 3 months. To serve: unwrap roll and cut into 2cm slices. Cut each slice into quarters. Place eight quarters in large ring on baking paper lined turntable. Microwave on 50% power for 1 to 3½ minutes or until just dry. Leave to cool for a minute on turntable, then remove to cake rack. Biscuits will crisp on cooling. Makes 7-8 dozen. If you wish to cook these biscuits they must be frozen first.

Warm citrus fruits in the microwave to extract more juice.

BAKING

• SPICED APPLE CAKE

1 granny smith apple
100 g butter
½ cup brown sugar
2 teaspoons cinnamon
1 teaspoon ground allspice

1 cup flour
½ teaspoon *Edmonds* baking powder
½ teaspoon baking soda
2 eggs

ICING:

½ teaspoon butter
½ teaspoon vanilla essence

1 cup icing sugar
Water

TOPPING:

1 teaspoon butter
1 tablespoon brown sugar

¼ cup chopped walnuts

Core and grate unpeeled apple. Put the butter in a two-litre glass microwave measuring jug. Microwave on High power (100%) for 1 minute or until melted. Add the sugar, cinnamon and allspice. Stir to dissolve the sugar. Add the apple. Sift flour, baking powder and soda. Fold dry ingredients into apple mixture. Add the eggs and beat until smooth. Pour batter into a 20cm microwave ring mould. Elevate and microwave on High for about 5 minutes or until surface is just springy to touch. Place an inverted plate on top of cake and allow to stand 2 minutes. Remove plate then allow to stand 5 minutes before unmoulding onto a cooling rack. When cold spread with icing then sprinkle with nut topping.

ICING:

Combine butter, vanilla and icing sugar. Gradually add sufficient water to form a thin icing.

TOPPING:

Put butter, brown sugar and walnuts in a microwave glass jug. Cook on High power for 2 minutes. Stir to mix then allow to harden.

• SPICED COFFEE CAKE

1 cup milk
1 tablespoon instant coffee
125 g butter
½ teaspoon baking soda
1¾ cups flour
2 teaspoons mixed spice

2 teaspoons *Edmonds* baking powder
¼ teaspoon salt
1½ cups sugar
2 eggs
1 tablespoon oil
Icing sugar

Put the milk, instant coffee and butter into a two-litre glass microwave measuring jug. Microwave on High power (100%) for 1½ to 2 minutes or until milk is heated and butter melted. Stir. Add soda, stirring to dissolve. Sift flour, mixed spice, baking powder and salt together. Add to melted ingredients along with sugar, eggs and oil. Beat to combine. Pour into a lightly greased 22cm cake mould. Elevate and microwave on High for 8 to 9 minutes or until just set. Allow to stand 5 minutes then unmould. When cold dust with icing sugar.

A watchful eye while microwave cooking is crucial.

• SPICED FRUIT ROLLUPS

1½ cups flour
100 g butter
2 teaspoons DYC dried yeast

1 tablespoon sugar
6 tablespoons tepid water
1 egg

FRUIT FILLING:

25 g butter
1 tablespoon sugar

1 teaspoon mixed spice
1 cup mixed fruit

Sift flour into a bowl and cut butter through until crumb-like. Combine yeast, sugar and water. Leave until frothy. Lightly beat egg. Add egg and yeast mixture to flour. Mix to form a smooth dough. Knead lightly. Put dough into a bowl or jug. Cover. Microwave on 30% power for 1 minute, leave 10 minutes. Repeat until dough has doubled in bulk. Punch down and lightly knead again. Roll dough out to a rectangle about 20cm x 30cm. Sprinkle with fruit mixture. Roll up like a sponge roll. Cut into nine even-sized pieces. Place eight pieces around the outside of a 20cm microwave cake dish. Place the remaining one in the centre. Elevate and microwave on 30% power for 1 minute, stand for 10 minutes. Repeat until dough has doubled in bulk. Microwave on High power (100%) for 3 minutes or until just set. Serve warm iced if wished.

FRUIT FILLING:

In a microwave bowl or jug put the butter, sugar and mixed spice. Microwave on High power for 1 minute or until butter has melted. Add the fruit, stir to moisten.

• SPICY MARBLE CAKE

100 g butter
¼ cup brown sugar
2 eggs
¾ to 1 cup milk
½ teaspoon baking soda
1 tablespoon oil

1½ cups flour
1 teaspoon *Edmonds* baking powder
2 teaspoons cinnamon
1 teaspoon ground nutmeg
1 teaspoon mixed spice
Icing sugar

Put the butter and sugar into a glass microwave measuring jug. Cover. Microwave on High power (100%) for 1 minute or until butter has melted. Beat in the eggs. Heat three-quarters of a cup of milk on High for 40 seconds or until hot. Add soda and stir to dissolve. Stir into the butter. Add the oil. Sift flour and baking powder. Beat into the melted ingredients. Add more milk if batter is too thick. Divide the batter in half. Add cinnamon, nutmeg and mixed spice to one half. Pour both batters alternately into a 20cm microwave ring mould. Run a skewer or knife through to marble. Elevate and cover with a paper towel. Microwave on High for 4½ minutes or until just springy to touch. Cake may still look wet in some areas. Stand for 5 minutes. Turn out onto a serving plate. Allow to go cold, then dust with icing sugar.

The denser the texture of a food the longer the cooking process carries on after food is taken from the oven.

BAKING

• SPICY APPLE MUFFINS

50 g butter
1 egg
½ cup milk
¾ cup brown sugar
2 medium apples
1 cup rolled oats

1 cup flour
2 teaspoons cinnamon
1 teaspoon mixed spice
1 teaspoon baking soda
½ teaspoon salt

Microwave butter in bowl or jug for approximately 1 minute or until melted. Add egg, milk and brown sugar. Core but do not peel apples. Grate coarsely and add to ingredients. Mix well. Add rolled oats and sifted dry ingredients. Stir till just combined. Half fill microwave muffin pans or paper cases with mixture. Microwave, elevated, on High power (100%) for 5 muffins 2 minutes; 6 muffins 2 minutes 30 seconds.

• SPONGE

3 eggs
½ cup oil
½ cup warm water
½ teaspoon vanilla essence
1 ¾ cups flour

3 teaspoons *Edmonds* baking powder
1 ½ cups castor sugar
About ¼ cup jam
¾ cup whipped cream
Icing sugar

Separate the eggs. Beat the egg yolks, oil, water and vanilla together. Sift the flour and baking powder into a mixing bowl. Stir in the sugar. Add the egg yolk mixture. Beat with an electric beater for about 4 minutes or until smooth. Beat egg whites until stiff but not dry. Carefully fold egg whites into the batter until well combined. Pour half the cake batter into a lightly greased 18cm shallow microwave cake pan. Microwave on High power (100%) for about 2½ minutes. Cake may be a little sticky to touch on the surface. Leave to stand 5 minutes. Turn out onto a cooling rack. Repeat with remaining batter. When cold fill with jam and cream. Dust with icing sugar.

NOTE: This sponge will be slightly denser than one cooked conventionally.

• SULTANA AND WALNUT LOAF

50 g butter
150 mls milk
½ cup brown sugar
½ cup sultanas
1 teaspoon vanilla essence
1 egg

1 ½ cups flour
2 teaspoons *Edmonds* baking powder
½ teaspoon cinnamon
1 teaspoon mixed spice
½ cup chopped walnuts

Put butter and milk into a glass microwave measuring jug. Microwave on High power (100%) for about 1 minute, or until butter has melted. Stir in sugar, sultanas and vanilla. Add the egg, beating to combine. Sift flour, baking powder, cinnamon and mixed spice. Gently fold in the sifted ingredients and walnuts. Pour batter into a 20cm microwave loaf pan. Cover with a paper towel. Microwave on 90% power for 6 to 8 minutes or until just set. Stand for 5 minutes.

Don't be afraid to open the microwave oven door and check cooking.

• SULTANA PECAN CAKE

¾ cup chopped pecans or walnuts
1 cup sultanas
1 teaspoon baking soda
½ teaspoon salt
1 tablespoon golden syrup
¾ cup boiling water

3 tablespoons butter
1 cup sugar
½ teaspoon vanilla
1½ cups flour
2 eggs

Combine nuts, sultanas, baking soda, salt and golden syrup in large bowl or jug. Add butter and boiling water, stir lightly and leave to stand 20 minutes. Add sugar and vanilla and mix well. Add flour and lightly beaten eggs and stir until thoroughly combined. Pour into medium-sized ring mould, elevate, cover with a sheet of paper towel and microwave on 75% power for 9-11 minutes. Stand 5 minutes and turn out. Serve warm or cold, with or without butter.

• SULTANA RING

1 cup sultanas
2 tablespoons butter
½ cup brown sugar
1 dessertspoon golden syrup
¼ teaspoon salt

1 cup water
1 teaspoon baking soda
1½ cups flour
1 teaspoon *Edmonds* baking powder

Put sultanas, butter, sugar, syrup and water in a bowl and microwave on High power (100%) for 2 minutes. When butter is melted add soda then sift in flour and baking powder and mix. Pour into a 20cm ring mould, cover with waxed paper and microwave on High power for about 4 minutes.

• TROPICAL CAKE

¾ cup milk
½ cup coconut
227 g can crushed pineapple
50 g butter
¾ cup sugar

2 eggs
½ teaspoon vanilla essence
1½ cups flour
2 teaspoons *Edmonds* baking powder

ICING:

1 teaspoon butter
1½ cups icing sugar

2 tablespoons passionfruit pulp

Combine milk and coconut. Leave to soak about 15 minutes. Drain the pineapple well. Put the butter and sugar in a large two-litre glass microwave measuring jug. Cover. Microwave on High power (100%) for 1 minute or until butter has melted. Add the eggs, vanilla, drained pineapple and coconut mixture. Beat to combine. Sift flour and baking powder. Fold sifted ingredients into measuring jug until just combined. Lightly grease a 20cm microwave ring mould. Elevate and microwave on High for about 6 minutes or until top surface is just set. Cover with a paper towel and leave to stand 5 minutes before turning out onto a cooling rack. When cold ice with passionfruit icing.

ICING:

Put butter and icing sugar into a bowl. Gradually add passionfruit pulp, mixing to a soft runny icing. Use to ice the cake.

Chocolate melted in the microwave holds its shape until mixed.

• WHOLEMEAL SHORT PASTRY FOR SAVOURY DISHES

1 cup wholemeal flour
1 teaspoon *Edmonds* baking powder
½ cup *Flemings* oat bran
100 g butter

¾ cup grated tasty cheese
1 egg yolk
About 3 tablespoons milk

Sift flour and baking powder into mixing bowl. Add the oat bran. Stir to combine. Cut butter through until it resembles fine breadcrumbs. Mix in cheese. Add egg yolk and sufficient milk to form a soft pliable dough. Wrap and chill for 15 minutes. Use as required. To make a flan base roll out and line a 20 cm flan dish. Prick the base. Elevate and cook on High power (100%) for 5 to 7 minutes or until pastry looks dry and blistered.

Use the microwave to soften cream cheese, butter and ice-cream for easier use in some recipes.

• AFGHANS

1 packet *Edmonds* Chocolate Cake Mix   3 cups cornflakes
50 g melted butter   3 tablespoons water

Combine all ingredients to form a stiff dough. Press into 23 x 30 cm microwave dish and smooth with the back of a spoon. Elevate and microwave on High power (100%) about 5½ minutes. Cut when cool. Ice with chocolate icing if wished.

VARIATION: For Peanut Brownies use 1 cup roughly chopped peanuts instead of cornflakes.

• BANANA CAKE

½ cup water
1 teaspoon instant coffee
1 tablespoon butter
2 bananas

1 packet *White Wings* Golden
   Butter Cake Mix
1 tablespoon milk
1 egg

Place water in a bowl and microwave on High power (100%) for 1 minute. Add coffee, butter and bananas and mash together with a fork. Mix in cake mix, milk and egg then pour into a 20cm ring mould, cover with waxed paper and microwave on High for 4½-5½ minutes. Stand 30 seconds, invert onto a cake rack. Ice cold cake with lemon or chocolate icing if wished.

• BLACK AND TAN SQUARE

1 packet *Edmonds* Chocolate Cake Mix   ¼ cup water
50 g melted butter   1 egg

FILLING:

½ tin sweetened condensed milk   25 g butter
1 tablespoon golden syrup

Mix cake mix, butter, water and egg and spread ⅔ of cake batter in a 23 x 30 cm microwave dish, cover with filling and dot with remaining batter. Elevate and microwave on High about 6 minutes. Cut when cool.

FILLING:

Combine condensed milk, golden syrup and butter. Microwave on High power (100%) for 1½ minutes, stir.

Cooking times will depend on the material of the cooking vessel. If you deviate from that specified in a recipe, the cooking time will probably differ.

• CHEESE AND ASPARAGUS SAVOURY

130 g packet *Edmonds* Ready Recipe
    Potato with Cheddar Cheese Sauce
310 g can asparagus spears
25 g butter
1½ cups warm water

½ cup reserved asparagus brine
100 mls milk
¼ cup cream
½ cup savoury toasted breadcrumbs
3 hard-boiled eggs

SAVOURY TOASTED BREADCRUMBS:

1 tablespoon butter
¾ cup soft breadcrumbs

1 tablespoon chopped fresh parsley
Freshly ground black pepper

Cook potatoes to packet directions. Drain the tin of asparagus, reserving half a cup of brine. Put the butter in a large microwave dish. Microwave on High power (100%) for 1 minute. Stir in the warm water and brine. Add potatoes, stir well then allow to stand for 5 minutes. Mix contents of sauce sachet with the milk. Cover with a lid or microwave-safe plastic wrap. Microwave on 70% power for 15 minutes. Stir every 5 minutes. Add the cream. Carefully put the asparagus spears over the potatoes. Continue cooking for another 3 to 5 minutes, or until potatoes are tender. Leave to stand 5 minutes. Peel and slice the eggs. Arrange egg slice on top of asparagus. Sprinkle the breadcrumbs on top. Serve immediately.
Serves 4-5.

SAVOURY TOASTED BREADCRUMBS:

Put the butter in a shallow microwave dish. Cover and microwave on High power (100%) for about 30 seconds. Add the breadcrumbs and parsley. Stir to combine. Microwave on High for 3 to 4 minutes or until browned, stirring frequently. Add the pepper.

• CHOCOLATE CHERRY GATEAU

1 pkt *Edmonds* Chocolate or Chocolate
    Butter Cake Mix
310 g tinned or fresh cherries

4 tablespoons sherry or brandy
300 ml cream
1 tablespoon icing sugar

Decoration: eg chopped walnuts or almonds, grated chocolate, jelly crystals, toasted coconut.
Prepare cake mix according to packet directions. When cold slice into 3 layers. Drain fruit and soak in brandy for about 1 hour. When ready to assemble, whip cream adding icing sugar and one tablespoon of the brandy in the final stage. Reserve some fruit to decorate the top, chop the rest and sprinkle half of it and the brandy over the bottom layer, spread with cream, put the next layer on top and repeat. Cover cake with cream, arrange fruit on top and decorate with nuts etc.

VARIATIONS: Use *Edmonds* Golden Yellow or Moist Orange Cake mixes with mandarins, apricots, kiwifruit etc.

• CHOCOLATE CHIP PUDDING WITH CHOCOLATE SAUCE

375 g packet *White Wings* Microwave
  Moist Chocolate Chip Cake Mix

SAUCE:

100 g cooking chocolate   ½ cup cream
25 g butter

Cook cake as directed on the packet. Serve as a dessert with Chocolate Sauce.

SAUCE:

Break chocolate into pieces and place in a microwave bowl. Add the butter. Cover and microwave on 70% power for 1 to 2 minutes or until chocolate has melted when stirred. Stir in the cream. Serve hot with Chocolate Chip Cake. Serves 6-8.

• CHOCOLATE FRUIT FLAN

375 g packet *White Wings* Microwave   425 g can sliced peaches
  Moist Chocolate Cake Mix   Glacé cherries

CUSTARD:

2 tablespoons *Edmonds* custard powder   ¾ cup milk
2 tablespoons sugar

Prepare cake mix as directed on the packet. Pour the batter into a 20cm microwave sponge flan dish. Elevate and microwave on High power (100%) for about 6 minutes or until cake shrinks slightly from the sides of the dish. Leave to stand 5 minutes before turning onto a cooling rack. Allow to go cold. Spread custard into the cavity. Drain peach slices. Arrange peaches decoratively on top of the custard. Garnish with glacé cherries. Serve as a dessert. Serves 6-8.

CUSTARD:

Combine custard powder and sugar. Mix to a smooth paste with a little of the measured milk. Gradually add remaining milk. Microwave on High power (100%) for 3 minutes, stirring every minute until custard is thick and bubbling. Cover and allow to cool.

• CHOCOLATE RASPBERRY SLICE

1 packet *Edmonds* Chocolate Cake Mix   ½ cup water
1 egg   Raspberry jam

Mix cake mix, egg and water with a spoon. Spread evenly in a 23cm ring mould, cover with a sheet of waxed paper and microwave on High power (100%) for about 4½ minutes. Cool slightly, spread with raspberry jam. When cool, cover with filling, allow to set then ice with chocolate icing.

FILLING:

50 g butter   1 cup icing sugar
1½ tablespoons boiling water   ½ teaspoon vanilla essence

Beat all ingredients until light and creamy.

◀ QUICK AND EASY EDMONDS MIXES Tangy Tuna Potatoes and Chocolate Fruit Flan.

37

QUICK AND EASY WITH EDMONDS MIXES

• COUNTRY STROGANOFF

130 g packet *Edmonds* Ready Recipe
   Potato with Country Mushroom
   Sauce
100 mls milk
1 cup cooked chicken meat

½ cup finely chopped onion
25 g butter
400 mls warm water
½ cup sour cream
2 teaspoons chopped fresh parsley

Empty sauce mix into a large microwave dish. Stir in the milk. Place half the potatoes into the dish. Top with chicken and onion. Arrange remaining potatoes on top. Add butter and warm water. Cover and microwave on High power (100%) for 20 minutes or until potatoes are tender. Pour the sour cream on top. Cook on High for a further 2 minutes. Serve garnished with parsley. Serves 4.

• DATE AND NUT CAKE WITH LEMON FROSTING

375 g packet *White Wings* Microwave
   Moist Date and Nut Cake Mix

LEMON FROSTING:

25 g butter
1 tablespoon water
1 tablespoon lemon juice

1 teaspoon grated lemon rind
1½ cups icing sugar

Cook cake to packet directions. Put the butter, water, lemon juice and rind into a microwave bowl. Microwave on High power (100%) for 2 minutes or until boiling. Sift icing sugar. Stir icing sugar into heated ingredients. Beat well. Spread on top of cake. Allow frosting to cool.

• DATE CARAMEL BARS

1 packet *White Wings* Golden Butter
   Cake Mix
1 cup chopped dates

50 g butter
¼ cup water
1 egg

Warm dates, butter and water together microwave on High power (100%) for 2 minutes then cool. Place icing ingredients in a large bowl and microwave on High 3½ minutes, cool. Add cake mix and egg to dates, mix and spread into a 23 x 30 cm microwave dish. Elevate and microwave on High about 5 minutes. Ice when icing and base are cool. When icing is half set cut with a hot knife.

ICING:

1½ cups brown sugar
2 tablespoons butter
¼ cup milk

Always choose a time option that undercooks the food cooked in the microwave. It is simple to add time to complete cooking.

• EVES CAKE

375 g packet *White Wings* Microwave
    Moist Sultana Buttercake
½ cup stewed apple
½ teaspoon mixed spice
1 tablespoon icing sugar

Prepare the cake as directed on the packet. Put the apple in a food processor with mixed spice. Purée until smooth. Fold apple into cake mix. Pour batter into a 20cm ring mould. Elevate and microwave on High power (100%) for about 6 minutes or until cake has shrunk slightly from the sides of the pan. Allow to stand 2 to 3 minutes before turning onto a cooling rack. Serve dusted with icing sugar.

• GOLDEN LEMON COCONUT CAKE

1 packet *White Wings* Golden Butter
    Cake Mix
1 egg
½ cup water
1 cup coconut

Mix ingredients with a spoon. Spread evenly in a 23 cm ring mould, cover with a sheet of waxed paper and microwave on High power (100%) about 4½ minutes.

When cake is cool ice with lemon icing and sprinkle grated lemon rind on top.

LEMON CREAM ICING:

1 cup icing sugar
3 tablespoons lemon juice
75 g soft butter

Beat sugar, lemon juice and butter until light and creamy.

• HEARTY CHICKEN AND RICE SOUP

1 large carrot
1 onion
2 stalks celery
25 g butter
1 packet Savoury Chicken Rice
    Risotto
4 cups boiling water
½ to ¾ cup diced cooked chicken

Peel and dice the carrot. Peel and chop the onion. Slice the celery. Put the carrot, onion, celery, butter and rice sachet in a large microwave dish. Cover and microwave on High power (100%) for 5 minutes, stirring after 2 minutes. Add the flavour sachet and boiling water, stir to mix. Microwave uncovered for 15 minutes, turning the dish halfway through cooking time. Add the chicken. Stir, leave to stand 2 minutes. Serve immediately.
Serves 4.

NOTE: On standing, rice will absorb more liquid so make just before required.

For foods that have thick and thin ends such as some fish, broccoli and chicken pieces, place the thickest part to the outside of the dish.

QUICK AND EASY WITH EDMONDS MIXES

• HOT SPANISH SALAD

400 g can whole tomatoes in juice
1 packet Barbeque Rice Risotto
400 g can whole kernel corn

1 green pepper
2 spring onions

Drain the tomatoes reserving the juice. Make up to 500ml with boiling water and use as the liquid to cook the Rice Risotto. Cook the Risotto according to the microwave directions on the packet. Drain the corn. Chop the tomatoes roughly. Deseed and cut the green pepper into strips. Finely chop the spring onions. Mix the tomatoes, corn and pepper into the rice mixture. Cook for 1 minute on High power (100%) or until heated through. Serve sprinkled with spring onions.
Serves 6.

• ITALIAN TATTIES

130 g packet *Edmonds* Ready Recipe
   Potato with Tomato and Savoury Onion
Sauce
1 cup tomato juice

1 teaspoon sugar
1½ cups cooked mince or
   leftover casserole

Follow preparation directions on the Ready Recipe packet. Replace one cup of liquid with tomato juice. Stir the sugar into the liquid. Cook as directed. Five minutes before end of cooking time stir in the mince or casserole mixture. Continue cooking until potato is tender. Serve hot.
Serves 4.

• JAFFA LAMINGTONS

1 packet *Edmonds* Moist Orange Cake Mix

Microwave cake according to packet directions.

DIP:

1 packet *Edmonds* Orange Jelly
1 tablespoon cocoa

½ cup boiling water

Mix jelly crystals and cocoa, add boiling water and stir till dissolved. When cake and dip are cool, cut cake into 2 layers and then into cubes or fingers, dip into jelly (using a fork) and roll in coconut. Leave to set.

Only use plastics designed for microwave use. Many plastics contain impurities and cannot be used safely in the microwave.

Warm brandy in the microwave before igniting for flambé dishes.

• JAFFA SLICE

1 packet *Edmonds* Moist Orange Cake Mix
1 egg
150mls water
1 tablespoon oil

Put cake mix in a mixing bowl. Beat together egg, water and oil. Add egg mixture to the cake mix. Mix with a fork for about 1 minute or until combined. Lightly grease a 22cm x 30cm microwave glass slice dish. Elevate. Cover loosely with a paper towel. Microwave on High power (100%) for about 5 minutes or until slice is cooked but still looks a little wet on top. Allow to cool in the tray. When cold spread with chocolate topping. Refrigerate until topping is set. To serve cut into fingers.

TOPPING:
150g cooking chocolate
½ cup low fat sour cream

Break the chocolate into a microwave bowl. Microwave on High power (100%) for about 1½ minutes. Stir every 30 seconds until melted. Combine melted chocolate and sour cream.

• JIFFY FRUIT TOPPED CHEESECAKE

50 g butter
1 packet *White Wings* Cheesecake mix
½ teaspoon cinnamon
1 cup milk
½ cup fruit juice or water
2 tablespoons sugar
1 tablespoon *Fielders* cornflour
Fresh or canned fruit

Melt butter, add crumb sachet and cinnamon and microwave on High power (100%) for 2 minutes. Press into 20 cm dish. Freeze whilst preparing filling. Make filling as per directions, pour over base and chill until set. Blend fruit juice, sugar and cornflour and heat on High for about 2 minutes stirring after 1 minute. Arrange fruit (eg. peaches, bananas, pineapple, kiwifruit) on top of cheesecake. Chill until served.

• LEMON SURPRISE DESSERT

1 packet *White Wings* Golden Buttercake Mix
2 teaspoons grated lemon rind
1 egg
150 mls water
1 tablespoon oil
3 cups vanilla ice-cream
2 teaspoons grated lemon rind
¼ cup chocolate chips
Icing sugar

Put the cake mix in a mixing bowl. In a bowl mix together the first measure of lemon rind, egg, water and oil. Add to the cake mix. Beat together with a fork for about 1 minute or until combined. Pour batter in a 20cm microwave ring mould. Elevate. Cover with a paper towel. Microwave on High power (100%) for about 6 minutes or until cake is cooked but still looks a little wet on top surface. Leave in mould for 5 minutes before turning onto a cooling rack. Allow to go cold. Cut top quarter off the cake. Carefully remove this portion. Cut out centre of cake, leaving the base and sides intact. (Use cake for cake crumbs in another recipe.) Freeze cake for 1 hour. Soften ice-cream in microwave on 30% power for about 1 minute. Stir in the second measure of lemon rind and chocolate chips. Spoon ice-cream into the cavity. Replace the piece of cake. Return the cake to the deep freeze. Freeze until firm. Dust with icing sugar before serving. Leave at room temperature for about 15 minutes before serving. Serve sliced with a chocolate sauce.

QUICK AND EASY WITH EDMONDS MIXES

• MICROWAVE RICE RING

1 packet Savoury Vegetable Rice Risotto   ½ cup chopped parsley
3 eggs

Cook the Rice Risotto to packet directions. Cool. Separate the eggs and add yolks and parsley to the rice. Beat the egg whites until stiff. Fold rice mixture into egg whites. Place in a 19cm microwave ring pan. Cover with microwave-safe plastic wrap and cook on High power (100%) for 4 minutes or until the mixture looks dry on top. Stand for three minutes before serving.
Serves 4-6.

• MICROWAVE RISOTTO TACOS

1 packet Mexican Style Rice Risotto   2 cups grated cheese
4 tomatoes   Shredded lettuce
10 to 12 taco shells   Chilli sauce

Cook the Rice Risotto as directed for the microwave instructions. Chop the tomatoes into small pieces. Heat the taco shells four at a time in the microwave on High power (100%) for 30 seconds, or until warm. Place about 2 table-spoons of cheese in the bottom of each taco shell. Top with Rice Risotto, chopped tomato and shredded lettuce. Pour over a little chilli sauce.
Makes 10-12.

• QUICK QUICHE

2 to 3 rashers bacon   3 eggs
1 onion   ½ cup soft breadcrumbs
½ green pepper   1 cup *Edmonds* pikelet or pancake
1 tablespoon butter   mix
¾ cup grated tasty cheese   2 tablespoons grated cheese
¾ cup milk

Derind bacon and chop the flesh. Peel and roughly chop the onion. Dice the green pepper. Put the butter in a glass microwave jug. Cover and microwave on High power (100%) for 30 seconds or until melted. Add the bacon, onion and green pepper. Microwave on High for 3 minutes. Spoon mixture into a microwave quiche or flan dish. Top with first measure of grated cheese. Microwave milk on High for 40 seconds. Beat milk and eggs together. Add breadcrumbs and pikelet mix. Mix until smooth. Pour pikelet mixture into flan dish. Microwave on 50% power for about 4 to 6 minutes or until set. Sprinkle with second measure of cheese. Place under grill. Grill until browned and top is crisp.
Serves 6-8.

Every microwave oven is different. Treat cooking time given in a recipe as a guide NOT an absolute rule.

• RHUBARB DESSERT CAKE

1 packet *Edmonds* Chocolate Buttercake
1 egg
125 g sour cream
½ cup water

2 cups chopped rhubarb
1 tablespoon melted butter
⅓ cup sugar
1 teaspoon cinnamon

Chop rhubarb into 1cm long pieces. Blend cake mix, egg, sour cream and water with a spoon then add rhubarb. Mix butter, sugar and cinnamon. Spread topping in a 20cm ring mould, spoon batter evenly in, cover with a sheet of waxed paper and microwave on High power (100%) for 4½ minutes then on 50% power 5 minutes. Stand 2 minutes then invert onto serving plate. Serve hot or cold with whipped cream or icecream.

• RICH TOMATO RISOTTO

1 packet Bacon and Tomato Rice Risotto
25 g butter

1½ cups boiling water
440 g can savoury tomatoes

Place the rice, contents of flavour sachet and butter in a microwave dish. Pour boiling water in dish, stir to mix. Microwave uncovered on High power (100%) for 8 minutes. Add savoury tomatoes, stir to combine. Turn the dish, then continue cooking for a further 5 minutes. Leave to stand 3 minutes before serving.
Serves 4-6.

• RUM BUTTERED SLICE

1 packet *Edmonds* Family Recipe
    Chocolate Cake Mix
1 egg

150 mls water
1 tablespoon oil

TOPPING:
25 g butter
1½ cups icing sugar

1½ teaspoons instant coffee
2 teaspoons rum

Put the cake mix in a mixing bowl. Lightly beat together the egg, water and oil. Add to the cake mix. Beat together with a fork until well combined. Lightly grease a 22cm x 30cm microwave glass slice dish. Pour batter into prepared dish. Elevate. Cover loosely with a paper towel. Microwave on High power (100%) for 5 minutes or until slice is cooked but still looks a little wet on top surface. Allow to cool. When cold ice with rum butter topping. Refrigerate until topping is firm. Cut into slices to serve.

TOPPING:
Beat butter until soft. Sift icing sugar. Gradually beat the icing sugar into the butter. Combine coffee and rum. Add sufficient rum mixture to form a spreadable icing.

• SHEPHERDS RICE PIE

1 onion
1 clove garlic
1 tablespoon butter
2 teaspoons curry powder
500 g topside mince

2 tablespoons cornflour
1 tablespoon DYC soy sauce
1 packet Savoury Beef Rice Risotto
1 cup grated cheese

Peel the onion and chop roughly. Crush, peel and mash the garlic. Put the butter, onion, garlic and curry powder in a large microwave dish. Cover and microwave on High power (100%) for 3 minutes or until onion is clear. Crumble the mince into the dish. Cook on High for 6 minutes or until meat has lost its pinkness, stirring every two minutes to break up the mince. Drain any fat that may have accumulated. Mix the cornflour and soy sauce until smooth. Stir into the meat. Microwave uncovered for 4 to 5 minutes on High until thickened, stirring once or twice during cooking. Set aside. Cook Rice Risotto to packet directions. Spread rice on top of beef mixture. Sprinkle with grated cheese. Microwave on High for 3 minutes or until cheese melts and beef is hot.
Serves 4-6.

• SULTANA BUTTERCAKE WITH LEMON SAUCE

1 packet *White Wings* microwave moist
   sultana buttercake

SAUCE:
2 tablespoons cornflour
2 tablespoons sugar
2 teaspoons grated lemon rind

¼ cup lemon juice
1 cup water
2 teaspoons butter

Make cake as directed on the packet. Serve warm as a dessert with Lemon Sauce.
Serves 6 to 8.

SAUCE:
In a microwave one-litre measuring jug combine cornflour and sugar. Add lemon rind. Mix to a smooth paste with lemon juice. Gradually add the water. Microwave on High power (100%) for about 4 minutes or until thick. Stir after 2 minutes. Add the butter and stir until melted.

• SUPER SPONGE PUDDING

2 eggs
1 packet *White Wings* Self Saucing
   Sponge Pudding

4 tablespoons sugar
1 cup hot water

Separate eggs. Add 1 teaspoon sauce mix to egg whites. Add sponge mix and ¼ cup cold water to egg yolks. Beat 4 minutes at medium speed. Mix to smooth batter with spoon. Spread batter into a 23 cm microwave dish. Add remaining sauce mix to hot water, mix and pour gently onto the batter. While sponge is cooking beat egg whites till stiff, gradually beat in sugar. Microwave on High power (100%) about 4½ minutes. Cover with meringue and microwave on High for 2 minutes.

NOTE: This can be prepared in 4-5 pudding bowls using the same microwaving times.

• TANGY TUNA POTATOES

130 g *Edmonds* Ready Recipe Potato
   with Sour Cream, and Chive Sauce
185 g can tuna in oil
½ cup cream

½ teaspoon lemon rind
1 tablespoon lemon juice
Fresh chives for garnish

Follow preparation directions on the Ready Recipe packet. Drain the tuna and flake. Stir in the tuna, cream, lemon rind and juice. Cook on 70% power for a further 5 minutes. Serve garnished with fresh chives.
Serves 4.

• VEAL PAPRIKA WITH MUSHROOM RISOTTO

1 packet Savoury Mushroom Rice
   Risotto
2 to 3 slices schnitzel
1 tablespoon flour
1 onion
100 g button mushrooms

25 g butter
1 teaspoon paprika
½ cup chicken stock
¼ cup low fat sour cream
Chopped parsley for garnish

Cook Rice Risotto to packet directions. Pound or roll the schnitzel until very thin. Cut into 3mm wide strips. Coat in flour until all flour is used. Peel and slice the onion. Wash and slice the mushrooms. Melt the butter in a large microwave dish. Add the onion, mix to coat with butter. Cover and cook on High power (100%) for 4 minutes. Add the mushrooms, meat and paprika., Stir, cover and cook 3 to 4 minutes or until meat loses its pinkness. Add chicken stock, cook on High for 1 minute or until stock thickens. Stir in the sour cream. Heat through on 70% power for about 30 seconds. Garnish with parsley. Serve with Mushroom Risotto.
Serves 4.

• VEGETABLE CURRY

2 carrots
1 kumara
2 stalks celery
1 clove garlic

1 onion
25 g butter
1 packet Savoury Curry Rice Risotto
¼ cup peas

Peel and slice the carrots. Peel and dice the kumara. Slice the celery. Crush, peel and mash the garlic. Peel the onion and cut into six. Separate the layers. In a large microwave dish put the carrot, kumara, celery, garlic, onion and butter. Cover with microwave-safe plastic wrap. Microwave on High power (100%) for 6 minutes, stirring occasionally. Add the rice and contents of flavour sachet. Continue cooking following the microwave directions on the packet. Stir the peas through the rice during standing time. Serve hot.
Serve 4-6.

Prick foods with skins such as sausages, potatoes and tomatoes. This will help stop skins bursting and prevent the food exploding in the microwave.

• ALL IN ONE CHOPS

1 potato	2 lamb shoulder chops
1 onion	1 tablespoon DYC mint sauce
1 carrot	¼ cup plum sauce
1 tomato	¼ cup green herb stock
1 tablespoon butter	1 teaspoon *Fielders* cornflour

Peel and cube the potato. Peel and slice the onion. Peel and slice the carrot. Cut the tomato into wedges. Put the butter in a microwave casserole dish. Cover and microwave on High power (100%) for 1 minute or until melted. Add the potato, onion, carrot and tomato, stir to coat in butter. Microwave on High for 2 minutes. Trim excess fat from meat. Brush the chops with mint sauce. Leave for 5 minutes. Arrange chops on top of vegetables. Combine the plum sauce, stock and cornflour. Spoon mixture over the chops. Cover and microwave on 70% power for 5 minutes. Turn chops over then microwave on 50% power for about 10 minutes, or until chops are tender. Serve hot.
Serves 1.

• APRICOT LAMB

1 lamb thick flank weighing about 250 g	½ cup soft breadcrumbs
1 spring onion	2 teaspoons DYC soy sauce
2 dried apricots	

Trim excess fat from meat. Finely chop the spring onion and apricots. Combine onion, apricots and breadcrumbs. Make a slit in the centre of the meat. Spoon crumb mixture into cavity. Brush the lamb with soy sauce. Place meat on a trivet and set on a microwave dish. Microwave on 50% power for 15 minutes; turn over after 10 minutes. Cover with foil shiny side down. Leave to stand 10 minutes. Serve half sliced for one meal. Make Eastern Lamb (page 48) with remaining meat.
Serves 1.

• BACON WITH VEGETABLE FRITTATA

1 onion	2 teaspoons chopped fresh parsley
1 tablespoon butter	2 teaspoons chopped fresh chives
1 cup cooked vegetables such as carrot, beans, courgette, cauliflower	Salt
	Freshly ground black pepper
2 eggs	2 slices ham
2 tablespoons milk	

Peel and finely chop the onion. Put the butter and onion in a glass microwave jug. Cover and microwave on High power (100%) for 2 minutes, stirring after 1 minute. Add the vegetables. Microwave on 70% power for 1 minute. Beat the eggs and milk together. Stir in the parsley, chives, salt and pepper. Stir to combine. Pour mixture into a shallow round glass microwave dish, redistributing the vegetables if necessary. Microwave on 70% power for 4 minutes or until just set. Carefully slide on to a serving plate. Serve with slices of ham.
Serves 1.

• BAKED APPLE

1 granny smith apple
1 tablespoon brown sugar
2 teaspoons *Flemings* rolled oats

2 tablespoons chopped dried apricots
1 teaspoon chopped walnuts
½ teaspoon butter

Core the apple, making sure all core is removed. Cut a sliver of apple from the base to make the apple more stable. Combine the sugar, oats, apricots and walnuts. Spoon mixture into the cavity. Dot with the butter. Cover with vented microwave-safe plastic wrap. Microwave on High power (100%) for 2 minutes or until apple is just tender. Leave to stand 1 minute. Serve hot.
Serves 1.

NOTE: If some of the filling should come out during cooking, spoon back into cavity before serving.

• BAKED BEAN SAVOURY

2 rashers bacon
1 onion
1 teaspoon butter

225 g can baked beans
2 eggs

Remove rind from the bacon and dice the flesh. Peel and finely chop the onion. Put the butter in a microwave jug. Microwave on High power (100%) for 40 seconds or until melted. Add the bacon and onion. Microwave on High for 1 minute or until onion is soft. Add the baked beans. Spoon mixture into a shallow microwave dish. Beat eggs with a fork. Pour on top of beans. Microwave on 50% power for about 4 minutes or until set. Sprinkle with topping. Serve hot.
Serves 1.

TOPPING:

1 teaspoon butter
½ cup soft breadcrumbs

2 teaspoons grated parmesan cheese

Microwave butter on High power (100%) for about 30 seconds or until melted. Add breadcrumbs, stir to combine. Microwave on High for about 2 minutes or until golden, stir occasionally during cooking. Add the parmesan, stirring to combine.

• CAULIFLOWER TOPPED POTATO

1 potato
½ cup cauliflower florets
¼ green pepper
1 spring onion
2 teaspoons lemon juice

1 teaspoon oil
¼ teaspoon wholegrain mustard
Salt
Freshly ground black pepper
2 teaspoons butter

Scrub the potato. Prick the skin several times with a fork. Microwave on High power (100%) for 3 to 5 minutes or until just soft when pressed. Turn over after 2 minutes cooking time. Leave to stand 4 minutes. While potato is standing tightly pack the cauliflower florets in a microwave dish. Add a table-spoon of water and microwave on High for about 3 minutes or until cooked. Finely chop the green pepper and spring onion. Combine cauliflower, green pepper and onion. In a screw top jar combine the lemon juice, oil, mustard, salt and pepper. Pour dressing over cauliflower mixture. Cut the top off the potato. Scoop out the centre. Mash with the butter. Return the potato to the shell. Top with cauliflower mixture. Serve any remaining cauliflower separately.
Serves 1.

• CRAB STICK OMELET

2 crab sticks	2 tablespoons milk
4 mushrooms	Salt
1 spring onion	Freshly ground black pepper
1 tablespoon butter	¼ cup bean sprouts
2 eggs	1 tablespoon grated cheese

Slice the crab sticks. Wipe and slice the mushrooms. Peel and finely chop the spring onion. Put the butter, mushrooms and onion into a microwave dish. Microwave on High power (100%) for 2 minutes, stirring after 1 minute. Lightly beat the eggs and milk. Season with salt and pepper. Stir in the egg mixture, crab sticks and bean sprouts. Sprinkle with cheese. Microwave on 70% power for 1 minute, stir, then continue cooking for about 3 minutes or until just set. Carefully turn onto a serving plate. Serve with crisp green salad. Serves 1.

• EASTERN LAMB

½ quantity cooked apricot lamb (page 46)	1 or 2 large Lebanese bread
2 teaspoons chopped fresh mint	Cucumber slices
About 2 tablespoons unsweetened natural yoghurt	Shredded lettuce
Freshly ground black pepper	Tomato slices

Thinly slice the lamb then cut into bite-sized pieces. Combine lamb, mint, yoghurt and pepper. Leave 15 minutes then microwave on 50% power for 40 seconds. Split the Lebanese bread, separate the two layers. Replace the layers. Place bread on a paper towel. Microwave on High power (100%) for 20 seconds or until soft. Spoon the meat down one edge of the bread. Add cucumber, lettuce and tomato. Roll up like a sponge roll. Serves 1.

• EVES PUDDING

5 tablespoons flour	1 egg
½ teaspoon *Edmonds* baking powder	Milk
1 tablespoon brown sugar	½ cup stewed apple
1 tablespoon *Flemings* oat bran	Icing sugar
25 g butter	

Sift flour and baking powder into a mixing bowl. Add sugar and oat bran, mix to combine. Put butter in a small microwave jug. Cover and microwave on High power (100%) for 1 minute, or until melted. Lightly beat the egg. Add the egg and butter to the dry ingredients. Stir to combine. Add milk if necessary to give a soft dropping consistency. Spoon the apple into the base of a small microwave ramekin dish. Smooth over top surface. Spoon batter evenly on top of apple. Elevate and microwave on 70% power for about 2 minutes or until just set. Dust with icing sugar. Serve with *Edmonds* custard if wished. Serves 1.

A watchful eye while microwave cooking is crucial.

• FISHERMANS PIE

1 fillet lemon fish, about 200 g
¼ cup finely chopped onion
1 tablespoon butter
1 tablespoon flour
¼ cup milk

2 teaspoons lemon juice
Salt
Freshly ground black pepper
2 tablespoons grated cheese
1 cup cold mashed potato

Wipe the fish. Place fish in a shallow microwave plate. Cover and microwave on High power (100%) for about 1 minute or until fish whitens and flakes easily. Flake the fish. Set aside. Put the onion and butter in a microwave one-litre jug. Microwave on High for 2 minutes or until onion is cooked. Stir in the flour. Microwave on High for 1 minute. Gradually add the milk. Microwave on High for 3 minutes, stirring every minute. Stir in the lemon juice, salt and pepper. Add flaked fish. Transfer to an individual microwave proof dish. Add cheese to potato, stirring to combine. Spoon or pipe potato on top of fish. Microwave on High for 1 minute. Place under the grill to give a crisp golden finish.
Serves 1.

NOTE: If piping the potato, microwave on High power (100%) for about 30 seconds or until just heated through. This will soften potato making it easier to pipe.

• FRUIT MERINGUE

½ cup fresh or tinned fruit such as
    peaches, pears, apricots,
1 egg white

1 tablespoon sugar
Few drops vanilla essence
¼ teaspoon cinnamon

Spoon the fruit into an individual ramekin dish. Cover and microwave on High power (100%) for 30 seconds or until warmed. Beat egg white until stiff but not dry. Beat in the sugar. Add the vanilla. Spoon meringue on top of fruit. Microwave on High for 1 minute. Dust with cinnamon. Serve warm.
Serves 1.

• FRUITY CHICKEN CURRY

1 clove garlic
1 onion
1 tablespoon butter
1 teaspoon curry powder
1 single chicken breast
1 teaspoon flour

2 teaspoons tomato purée
½ cup chicken stock
1 tablespoon DYC spiced vinegar
1 cooking apple
1 tablespoon raisins
1 tablespoon chopped parsley

Crush, peel and mash the garlic. Peel and slice the onion. Put the butter in a microwave dish. Cover and microwave on High power (100%) for 1 minute, or until melted. Add the garlic, onion and curry powder. Microwave on High for 2 minutes. Add the chicken breast. Microwave on 70% power for 1½ to 2 minutes, or until juices run clear. Remove chicken and set aside. Stir in the flour and tomato purée. Cook on High for 1 minute. Stir in the chicken stock and vinegar. Return chicken to casserole. Peel, core and chop the apple. Add the apple and raisins. Microwave on 50% power for about 6 minutes, or until chicken is tender and apple soft, stirring occasionally during cooking. Serve on a bed of rice. Garnish with chopped parsley.
Serves 1.

MEALS FOR ONE

• MAIN MEAL CHICKEN SALAD

1 single chicken breast
2 cloves garlic
1 teaspoon DYC soy sauce
2 tablespoons oil
1 tablespoon DYC malt vinegar
1 tablespoon DYC white vinegar
1 teaspoon honey

1 carrot
1 stalk celery
1 small apple
¼ cup chopped gherkins
¼ cup undrained pineapple pieces
Lettuce leaves

Remove skin from chicken breast. Flatten between two pieces of plastic wrap. Crush, peel and mash the garlic. Combine garlic and soy sauce. Brush the breast with this mixture. Microwave on 70% power for 2 minutes or until juices run clear. Brush again after I minute with juices from the chicken. Cut chicken into slivers. Combine the meat juices, oil, vinegars and honey. Pour over the chicken and leave to cool. Peel and cut the carrot and celery into thin julienne strips. Core and dice the apple. Mix the carrot, celery, apple, gherkins and undrained pineapple with the chicken. Serve on a bed of lettuce.
Serves 1.

• MALLOW DELIGHT

6 marshmallows
¼ cup cream
1 tablespoon coconut

1 banana
1 teaspoon lemon juice

Halve the marshmallows. Combine marshmallows and cream. Microwave on 50% power for about 45 seconds to 1 minute, or until soft. Stir to combine. Add the coconut. Peel and slice the banana. Place in a serving dish. Spoon lemon juice over banana. Top with marshmallow mixture. Refrigerate until firm.
Serves 1.

• MUSTARD CHICKEN BREASTS

1 single boneless chicken breast
1 teaspoon butter
¼ cup dry white wine
1 tablespoon sour cream

¼ teaspoon wholegrain mustard
Salt
Freshly ground black pepper

Remove skin from chicken. Flatten the breast between two pieces of plastic wrap. Put butter in a shallow microwave dish. Cover and microwave on High power (100%) for 30 seconds or until melted. Coat the chicken with butter. Place the chicken in the dish and microwave on 70% power for 1 minute. Add the wine, cream and mustard. Microwave on 70% power for a further 2 minutes or until chicken is tender. Season with salt and pepper. Serve hot.
Serves 1.

When using the microwave for casseroles ensure all meat to be cooked is immersed in the liquid. If not, sit a plate on top to correct the problem. Use less liquid in casseroles than you would in conventional cooking.

• OAT CRUMBLE

2 stalks rhubarb
2 teaspoons sugar
3 tablespoons flour
2 tablespoons *Flemings* rolled oats

1 tablespoon coconut
2 tablespoons brown sugar
25 g butter

Trim, peel and cut the rhubarb into lcm pieces. Microwave on High power (100%) for 1½ minutes or until rhubarb is tender. Stir in the sugar. Spoon into an individual microwave serving dish. Set aside. Combine the flour, oats, coconut and brown sugar. Cut through the butter until crumb-like. Spoon crumble over rhubarb. Microwave on High for 2 minutes or until crumble is cooked.
Serves 1.

• OATY TOPPED FISH

1 tablespoon butter
½ teaspoon grated lemon rind
2 tablespoons *Flemings* rolled oats
¼ cup soft breadcrumbs
1 white fish fillet

1 tablespoon lemon juice
Salt
Freshly ground black pepper
1 tablespoon finely chopped spring onion

Put the butter in a shallow microwave dish. Cover and microwave on High power (100%) for 1 minute or until melted. Add the lemon rind, oats and bread crumbs. Stir to coat with butter. Microwave on High for 2 minutes. Set aside. Place the fish onto a serving plate. Cover with microwave-safe plastic wrap. Microwave on High for about 45 seconds or until fish is white and flakes easily. Spoon lemon juice, salt and pepper over the fish. Top with oaty topping. Garnish with spring onion.
Serves 1.

NOTE: Drain any juice off the plate directly after cooking the fish.

• ORANGE CARAMEL CUSTARD

1 tablespoon sugar
1 teaspoon water
½ cup milk
2 teaspoons sugar

1 teaspoon grated orange rind
1 egg
Orange segments to serve

Put the sugar and water into an individual microwave ramekin dish. Microwave on High power (100%) for 2 minutes or until sugar turns light golden in colour. Remove from microwave then tilt the dish to coat with caramel. Set aside. Put the milk into a glass microwave jug. Microwave on High for 40 seconds or until hot. Stir in the sugar and orange rind. Add egg and beat to combine. Pour into prepared dish. Microwave on 30% power for about 2 to 3 minutes or until just set. Refrigerate until firm. Unmould and serve with segments of orange.
Serves 1.

Small amounts of food cook better than large amounts in the microwave.

• ORANGE ROUGHY WITH LEMON

2 spring onions
¼ cup lemon juice
2 tablespoons cream
¼ teaspoon salt

¼ teaspoon freshly ground white pepper
1 fillet orange roughy
1 teaspoon capers

Finely chop the spring onions. Put the onions and lemon juice in a microwave dish. Microwave on High power (100%) for 1½ minutes or until onion is soft. Stir in the cream. Season with salt and pepper. Cover and set aside. Place the fish on a serving plate. Cover with microwave-safe plastic wrap. Microwave on High for about 45 seconds or until fish whitens and flakes easily. Spoon cream sauce over the fish. Garnish with capers. Serve hot.
Serves 1.

NOTE: Drain any juice off the plate directly after cooking the fish.

• POTATO AND KIDNEY FRY

1 medium potato
2 kidneys
1 rasher bacon

¼ medium onion
1 teaspoon clarified butter

Prick potato, cook on High power (100%) for 2 minutes or until almost cooked, slice thickly. Peel, halve and trim kidneys. Remove rind from bacon. Peel and slice the onion. Preheat browning dish for maximum suggested time. Add clarified butter and move dish to coat. Place potato, kidneys, bacon and onion in dish, allow to sizzle for a few seconds, turn and cook on High for 1 minute. Turn and cook on High for a further minute.
Serves 1.

• POTATO AND SILVERBEET FLAN

2 leaves silverbeet
1 cup hot mashed potato
1 tablespoon flour
Salt
Freshly ground black pepper

1 slice ham
¼ cup grated tasty cheese
2 eggs
2 tablespoons cream
About ½ teaspoon paprika

Wash the silverbeet, remove the white stem. Microwave leaves on High power (100%) for 1 to 1½ minutes or until cooked. Drain. Chop silverbeet finely. Combine silverbeet, potato and flour. Use to line the base and sides of a 10cm shallow microwave pie plate. Season with salt and pepper to taste. Chop the ham. Put the ham and cheese into the lined dish. Lightly beat eggs and cream together. Pour egg mixture over the ham. Microwave on 50% power for 5 minutes or until partially set. Spoon crumble topping over. Sprinkle with paprika. Microwave on 70% power for 3 minutes or until almost set in the centre. Allow to stand 3 minutes or until set. Serve with salad.
Serves 1.

TOPPING:

1 tablespoon butter
1 cup soft breadcrumbs

¼ cup *Flemings* oat bran

Put butter in a shallow microwave dish. Cover and microwave on High power (100%) for 1 minute or until melted. Add breadcrumbs and oat bran. Stir to coat. Microwave on High power (100%) for 2 minutes or until golden, stir during cooking.

• PUMPKIN SOUFFLÉ

2 rashers bacon	1 egg
1 tablespoon butter	¾ cup cold mashed pumpkin
1 tablespoon chopped onion	Salt
2 tablespoons flour	Freshly ground black pepper
½ cup milk	1/8 teaspoon ground nutmeg
¼ cup grated tasty cheese	

Derind bacon and chop the flesh. Put butter in a one-litre glass measuring jug. Cover and microwave on High power (100%) for 1 minute or until melted. Add onion and bacon and microwave on High for 1 minute. Stir in the flour, microwave for 1 minute. Gradually add the milk, stirring all the time. Microwave on High for about 3 minutes, stirring every minute. Leave to stand for 1 minute. Stir in the cheese. Separate the egg. Add the yolk to the sauce along with pumpkin, salt, pepper and nutmeg. Beat egg white until stiff but not dry. Carefully fold egg white into pumpkin mixture. Lightly grease a one-cup capacity ramekin or souffle dish. Pour mixture into prepared dish. Elevate and microwave on 50% power for about 6 minutes or until risen and just set. Allow to stand for 2 minutes. Serve with a crisp green salad.
Serves 1.

• QUICK LAMB PIE

Cooked roast lamb leftover from the roast	1 tablespoon tomato sauce
1 onion	Salt
2 teaspoons butter	Freshly ground black pepper
1 tablespoon mint sauce	Roast potato
¼ cup prepared gravy	¼ cup grated cheese

Put meat into a food processor or blender. Process until finely chopped. Peel and chop the onion. Put the butter and onion into a microwave jug. Cover and microwave on High power (100%) for 2 minutes, stir. Add onion to meat along with mint sauce, gravy and tomato sauce. Transfer to a small microwave casserole dish. Season with salt and pepper. Thinly slice the potato. Layer the potato over the meat. Microwave on High power for 1 to 2 minutes or until heated through. Sprinkle cheese on potato. Serve hot.
Serves 1.

• SAUCY DRUMSTICKS

2 chicken drumsticks	1 tablespoon chutney
2 teaspoons butter	1 teaspoon curry powder
1 teaspoon prepared mustard	½ teaspoon salt

Wipe the drumsticks with a paper towel. Put the butter in a microwave dish. Cover and microwave on High power (100%) for about 40 seconds or until melted. Stir in the mustard, chutney, curry powder and salt. Spread chicken drumsticks with this mixture. Place drumsticks on a shallow microwave dish. Arrange drumsticks so the meatiest part is to the outside of the dish. Microwave on High for 4 minutes, or until juices run clear when tested.
Serves 1.

◄ SOUPS Mild Curry Chicken and Alphabet Soup, Italian Mussel Soup and Lemon and Broccoli Soup.

MEALS FOR ONE

• ROAST LAMB WITH VEGETABLES

About 650 g fillet end leg of lamb
1 teaspoon prepared mustard
2 teaspoons DYC soy sauce
1 clove garlic
2 potatoes

1 kumara
1 piece pumpkin
1 teaspoon butter
Prepared microwave browning mix

Trim excess fat from meat. Combine mustard and soy sauce. Crush and peel the garlic. Cut the garlic into slivers. Push the slivers of garlic into cuts made in the meat. Brush meat with soy mixture. Place meat on a trivet inside a roasting bag. Microwave on High power (100%) for 5 minutes. Brush meat again with soy mixture. Microwave on 50% power for 10 minutes. Remove meat from the bag. Cover with aluminium foil, shiny side down and leave meat to stand for 10 minutes. (Serve half the meat sliced with one roast potato, vegetables and gravy.) Make a gravy from pan juices. Peel vegetables and cut into even-sized pieces. Wash well. Place vegetables into a microwave casserole dish with only the water that is clinging to them. Make sure the kumara is in the centre position. Microwave on High power for 5 to 6 minutes. Drain water from casserole. Add the butter and prepared microwave browning mix. Stir to coat. Cook on High for a further 5 minutes or until tender. Serves 1.
Use remaining meat and vegetables for Quick Lamb Pie (page 55).

• SAUSAGE AND KUMARA CASSEROLE

2 sausages
1 teaspoon DYC soy sauce
1 onion
1 small kumara
1 tablespoon butter

½ cup undrained pineapple chunks
¼ cup chicken stock
1 teaspoon *Fielders* cornflour
1 teaspoon DYC spiced vinegar

Prick the sausages. Brush with soy sauce. Place sausages in a small microwave casserole dish or brown paper bag. Microwave on High power (100%) for about 2 minutes or until cooked. Cut each sausage into four. Set aside. Peel and slice the onion. Peel the kumara and chop into even-sized pieces. Put the butter into a glass microwave casserole dish. Cover and microwave on High for 1 minute or until melted. Add the onion and kumara. Stir to coat the vegetables with butter. Microwave on High for 2 minutes or until onion is cooked and kumara is almost soft. Add the sausages, pineapple chunks and chicken stock. Mix the cornflour and vinegar to a smooth paste. Add this to the casserole. Cover and microwave on High for 2 minutes, stirring after 1 minute, or until juices thicken slightly. Serve on a bed of rice.
Serves 1.

NOTE: If you want the sausages browner, either brown them first in a pan, browning dish or grill.

Always elevate a roast — cook in an oven bag or covered dish. When roasting vegetables cut pumpkin larger than potato and set the kumara in the centre of the dish.

• SAVOURY CASES

1 bread roll
Butter
2 slices salami
1 spring onion
2 eggs

Salt
Freshly ground black pepper
1 tablespoon finely chopped green
 pepper
1 teaspoon chopped parsley

Cut the top off the bread roll. Scoop out the centre and use to make bread-crumbs for another dish if wished. Spread butter on the inside of the roll. Set on a ridged microwave plate. Microwave on High power (100%) for 40 sec-onds. Set aside. Cut the salami into thin strips. Finely chop the spring onion. Lightly beat the eggs, salt and pepper together. Add the salami, onion, and green pepper. Place the egg mixture into the bread roll. Microwave on High for 30 seconds. Stir well then continue to cook for about another 20 seconds or until egg increases in volume. Stir again then let stand for 30 seconds. Garnish with chopped parsley.
Serves 1.

NOTE: If egg is not quite cooked after second cooking time, continue cooking for 10 seconds, or at 10 second intervals until cooked.

• SAVOURY EGG POTS

2 tablespoons finely chopped green
 and red pepper
¼ diced spring onion
1 egg

2 tablespoons milk
Salt
Freshly ground black pepper
2 tablespoons grated cheese

Lightly grease an individual microwave ramekin dish or tea cup. Place diced pepper and spring onion into the base of prepared dish. Cover and microwave on High power (100%) for 1 minute. Lightly beat the egg and milk together. Season with salt and pepper. Pour egg mixture over the vegetables. Return to the microwave. Cover and cook on 70% power for about 50 seconds or until just set. Stand 1 minute. Invert onto a serving plate. Sprinkle with grated cheese. Serve with crisp green salad and a baked potato.
Serves 1.

• SHERRIED CHICKEN

1½ cups cooked chicken meat
¼ cup chopped green pepper
1 tablespoon dry sherry
2 spring onions

1 tablespoon butter
1 tablespoon flour
¼ cup milk
¼ cup chicken stock

Cut chicken into bite-sized pieces. Add green pepper. Pour sherry on top and leave to marinate about 15 minutes. Finely slice the spring onions. Put the butter in a microwave jug. Cover and microwave on High power (100%) for 1 minute or until melted. Stir in the flour. Microwave on High for 1 minute. Gradually stir in the flour, milk and stock. Microwave on High for 3 minutes or until sauce boils and thickens, stirring every minute. Add the chicken mixture to the sauce, stir to combine. Microwave on High for 1 minute. Serve on a bed of cooked Diamond pasta.
Serves 1.

MEALS FOR ONE

• TANGY BEEF

1 clove garlic
1 onion
¼ green pepper
200 g topside mince
2 teaspoons brown sugar
1 teaspoon *Fielders* cornflour

2 teaspoons DYC vinegar
¼ teaspoon salt
¼ teaspoon freshly ground black pepper
2 teaspoons DYC soy sauce
½ cup undrained pineapple chunks

Crush, peel and mash the garlic. Peel and slice the onion. Dice the pepper. Break mince into a small microwave casserole dish. Add onion and garlic. Microwave on High power (100%) for 4 minutes, or until mince loses its pinkness. Stir every minute to break up the meat. Drain any fat that may have accumulated. Stir in the green pepper. Combine the sugar, cornflour, vinegar, salt, pepper and soy sauce. Stir into the meat. Microwave uncovered for 3 to 4 minutes or until thickened. Stir in the pineapple. Serve on a bed of rice. Serves 1.

• TOMATO CHICKEN

1 onion
1 clove garlic
2 teaspoons butter
1 single chicken breast

225 g can tomato soup
1 cup frozen mixed vegetables
Freshly ground black pepper

Peel and slice the onion. Crush, peel and mash the garlic. Put butter, onion and garlic into a small glass microwave casserole dish. Cover and microwave on High power (100%) for 1 minute, stir. Place chicken breast on top of onion mixture. Microwave on 70% power for 1 ½ minutes. Pour contents of soup on top of chicken. Add mixed vegetables and pepper and continue cooking on 70% power for 3 minutes or until vegetables are hot. Serve on Diamond pasta. Serves 1.

• VEGETABLE MACARONI CHEESE

1 onion
1 tablespoon butter
1 tablespoon flour
1 cup milk
½ teaspoon prepared mustard
¼ cup grated tasty cheese
1 cup leftover vegetables

Salt
Freshly ground black pepper
1 cup cooked *Diamond* macaroni elbows
6 tomato slices
2 tablespoons toasted breadcrumbs

Peel and chop the onion. Put the onion and butter into a one-litre microwave jug. Cover and microwave on High power (100%) for 2 minutes. Stir in the flour and cook on High for a further 1 minute. Gradually add the milk, stirring all the time. Microwave on High for 3 minutes or until sauce boils, stirring every minute. Add mustard, cheese, vegetables, salt and pepper. Put half the macaroni on the base of a small casserole dish. Spoon half the sauce on top. Arrange half the tomato slices over. Repeat with remaining ingredients. Microwave on 70% power for 5 minutes or until heated through. Spoon toasted breadcrumbs on top just before serving. Serves 1,

The microwave can be used to dry herbs and flowers.

• CHICKEN STOCK

1 chicken carcass or 4 chicken backs
1 small onion
1 tablespoon butter
1 bayleaf

1 sprig thyme
1 sprig parsley
3 black peppercorns
1½ cups water

Quarter chicken carcass. Peel and roughly chop the onion. Melt the butter in a microwave dish on 50% power for 20 seconds. Add onion and chicken, cook on High power (100%) for 2 minutes. Add bayleaf, thyme, parsley, peppercorns and water. Cover. Microwave on High for 10 minutes or until stock boils. Stir. Microwave on 50% for 40 minutes. Strain, cool, then refrigerate. Remove the fat before using. Makes 1½ cups.

• CHUNKY VEGETABLE SOUP

2 carrots
2 stalks celery
1 onion
2 courgettes
1 small kumara
25 g butter

1½ teaspoons flour
½ cup tomato purée
5½ cups boiling chicken stock
½ cup finely chopped parsley
Salt and pepper

Scrub the carrots and dice. Wash and slice the celery. Peel and finely chop the onion. Wash and dice the courgettes. Peel and dice the kumara. In a large microwave dish melt the butter on 70% power for 20 seconds. Add the carrots, celery and onion and toss to coat with butter. Cover and cook on High power (100%) for 5 minutes. Add the flour, cook for 1 minute on High. Stir in the tomato purée. Gradually add the boiling stock. Add the courgettes, kumara and parsley. Cook for a further 5 minutes on High stirring halfway through cooking. Season with salt and pepper.
Serves 8.

• CREAM OF MUSHROOM SOUP

200 g mushrooms
2 spring onions
25 g butter
1½ tablespoons flour

1½ cups milk
½ teaspoon salt
Freshly ground black pepper

Wash and slice the mushrooms. Reserve one sliced mushroom for garnish. Finely chop the spring onions. Melt the butter in a microwave dish on 70% power for 20 seconds. Add the mushrooms and spring onions. Cook for 2 minutes on 90% power. Remove from the dish, set aside. Add the flour to the dish. Cook on High power (100%) for 1 minute. Gradually add the milk. Microwave on High for 3 minutes stirring after 2 minutes. Return the mushroom mixture to the dish. Purée the soup until smooth in a blender. Season with salt and pepper. Return the soup to the dish. Microwave on 70% for 2 minutes. Serve the soup garnished with mushroom slices.
Serves 4.

The flavour of microwave soups develops if left to stand so ideally it is better to make them the day before.

SOUPS

• CREAM OF CHICKEN AND VEGETABLE SOUP

1 onion
2 cloves garlic
1 stalk celery
1 large carrot
25 g butter
2 cups milk

¼ to ½ teaspoon ground mace
½ teaspoon salt
¼ teaspoon freshly ground black
    pepper
¼ teaspoon sugar

SAUCE:

1½ tablespoons butter
1½ tablespoons flour
2 cups milk

Peel and finely chop the onion. Crush, peel and mash the garlic. Wash and finely slice the celery. Peel and finely dice the carrot. Put the onion, garlic, celery, carrot and butter into a large microwave dish. Cover. Microwave on High power (100%) for 2 minutes. Stir to coat the vegetables thoroughly with melted butter. Cover. Cook on High for a further 4 to 5 minutes or until vegetables are tender. Add the stock and continue cooking for 2 minutes. Stir in the sauce and chicken. Season to taste with salt and pepper. Serve with croutons for garnish.
Serves 6.

SAUCE:

Put butter in a microwave glass measuring jug. Cover. Microwave on High power (100%) for 30 seconds until butter has melted. Stir in the flour, cook for a further minute. Gradually add the milk stirring all the time. Microwave on High for about 3 minutes or until sauce thickens and boils. Stir after 2 minutes.

• CREAM OF SPINACH SOUP

500 g bunch spinach
1 onion
2 cloves garlic
25 g butter
2 tablespoons flour
2 cups boiling chicken stock

2 cups boiling chicken stock
About 1 cup diced cooked chicken
    meat
Salt and pepper
Croutons for garnish

Wash the spinach leaves. Remove stems and discard. Put spinach in a microwave casserole dish. Cover. Microwave on High power (100%) for 3 minutes or until leaves have wilted but are still bright green. Set aside. Peel and chop the onion. Crush, peel and mash the garlic. Put the onion, garlic and butter into a microwave dish. Cover. Microwave on High for 2 minutes or until onion is tender. Stir in the flour and microwave for a further I minute. Gradually add the boiling stock, stirring all the time. Add the spinach leaves. Transfer to a food processor or blender. Blend until smooth. Return to casserole dish. Add the milk. Microwave on High for about 3 minutes until hot and thickened, stirring after each minute. Add mace, salt, pepper and sugar. Serve hot.
Serves 6.

Reheating a bowl of soup: Microwave on High power (100%) for 2 to 3 minutes stirring frequently. When using commercial stock powders use with a little restraint and season with salt and pepper to taste.

• CREAMED CELERY SOUP

1 onion
1 rasher bacon
1 tablespoon butter
5 stalks celery
2 cups hot chicken stock

1 tablespoon butter
1 tablespoon flour
1 cup milk
Salt and pepper

Peel and roughly chop the onion. Derind the bacon and chop the flesh. In a large microwave dish melt the first measure of butter on 50% power for 20 seconds. Add the onion and bacon. Microwave on High power (100%) for 1 minute. Wash and thinly slice the celery. Add to the dish. Microwave on High for 6 to 7 minutes or until the celery is tender. Add the hot chicken stock. Purée the celery and stock in a blender or sieve until smooth. Place second measure of butter in a one-litre glass jug. Microwave on High for 30 seconds, add the flour, cook 1 minute. Gradually add the milk to the jug stirring to combine. Cook on High for 3 minutes stirring after 2 minutes. Combine the white sauce and celery purée. Season with salt and pepper to taste. Cook on High for 1 to 2 minutes or until thoroughly heated through.
Serves 6.

• CURRIED PARSNIP SOUP

3 parsnips
1 onion
2 teaspoons clarified butter

1 teaspoon curry powder
2¼ cups boiling chicken stock

Trim and peel the parsnips. Cut into 1cm thick slices. Peel and roughly chop the onion. In a microwave dish melt the butter on 50% power for 20 seconds. Add the onion and toss to coat in butter. Cook on High power (100%) for 2 minutes. Add the curry powder, cook on High for 1 minute. Stir in the sliced parsnips and chicken stock. Cover and cook on High for 6 minutes or until parsnips are tender. Purée in a blender until smooth.
Serves 4 to 6.

• DHAL SOUP

1 to 2 teaspoons minced fresh chilli
1 cup red lentils
3 cups boiling water
2 cloves garlic
1 onion

1 tablespoon butter
1 teaspoon cumin
1 teaspoon grated root ginger
1 tablespoon lemon juice
Salt

Put the chilli, lentils and water into a microwave glass bowl. Microwave on High power (100%) for about 20 minutes or until lentils are soft. Mash slightly. Crush, peel and mash the garlic. Peel and finely chop the onion. In a small measuring jug put the butter, garlic, onion, cumin and ginger. Microwave on High for 2 to 3 minutes or until soft. Add onion mixture and lemon juice to lentils. Microwave on High for 1 minute or until hot. Season with salt.
Serves 4.

NOTE: The spiciness of this soup will depend on the amount of chilli used; it also requires quite a bit of salt.

SOUPS

• FISH CHOWDER

3 tablespoons butter	2 stalks celery
Fish head and bones	200 g white fish fillets
1 onion	1 tablespoon flour
2 cups cold water	1 cup milk
1 bayleaf	Salt and pepper
6 black peppercorns	2 tomatoes
1 large potato	1 tablespoon finely chopped parsley
1 onion	

In a microwave dish heat one tablespoon of measured butter on 70% power for 20 seconds. Wash the fish head and place with the bones in the dish. Peel the onion and cut into six. Put onion in a microwave dish. Cover. Cook on High power (100%) for 5 minutes. Add the water, bayleaf and peppercorns. Cover and microwave on High for 5 minutes or until water boils. Reduce heat to 70% for 5 minutes. Allow stock to stand 5 minutes then strain. Peel the potato and cut into 8mm cubes. Peel and finely chop the onion. Wash and slice the celery. In a large microwave dish add one tablespoon of measured butter, melt on 70% for 20 seconds. Add the potato, onion and celery, toss to coat the vegetables with butter. Cover and microwave on High for 5 minutes. Cut fish into bite-sized pieces and add with the reserved stock to the vegetables. Cook on High for 2 minutes. Set aside. Heat the remaining butter in a one-litre glass jug on 70% for 20 seconds. Add the flour, cook on High for 1 minute. Gradually add the milk stirring to combine. Microwave on High for 3 minutes stirring after 2 minutes. Add the sauce to the fish mixture, mixing well to combine. Microwave on 90% for 2 minutes. Season with salt and pepper. Dice the tomatoes and add with the parsley. Serve as a meal.
Serves 5 to 6.

• FISH STOCK

1 fish head, bones and skin	6 peppercorns
¼ onion	1 cup water
1 bayleaf	

Wash the fish head and put in a medium-sized microwave jug or bowl. Add bones and skin, onion, bayleaf, peppercorns and water. Microwave on High power (100%) for 5 minutes or until liquid boils. Reduce heat to 50% power, cook for a further 5 minutes. Strain.
Makes about 1 cup.

• FRENCH BREAD CROUTONS

25 g butter	1 French bread stick
31 g packet onion soup mix	

Soften the butter, mix the soup mix into the butter. Allow mixture to stand for at least one hour. Cut the French bread into thin slices. Butter each slice with the flavoured butter. Place on a paper towel in a microwave. Allow 12 to 14 seconds on High power (100%) per slice. Serve with soups.

Reheating a bowl of soup: Microwave on High power (100%) for 2 to 3 minutes stirring frequently. When using commercial stock powders use with a little restraint and season with salt and pepper to taste.

• FRENCH ONION SOUP

3 onions
1 clove garlic
50 g butter
2 teaspoons flour

1½ cups boiling beef stock
1½ cups boiling water
¼ cup dry red wine

Peel and finely slice the onions. Crush, peel and mash the garlic. In a large microwave dish melt the butter on 70% power for 30 seconds. Add the sliced onions and garlic. Cover and cook on High power (100%) for 8 to 10 minutes until onions are soft, stirring occasionally. Stir in the flour and cook on High for 20 seconds. Stir in the beef stock, water and red wine. Microwave on High for 2 minutes. Serve with a cheese crouton.
Serves 6.

CROUTONS:

¼ cup grated cheese
6 slices French bread

¼ teaspoon paprika

Divide the grated cheese evenly among the slices of bread. Sprinkle each bread slice with paprika. Place the slices of bread on a paper towel in the microwave. Microwave on High for 50 seconds.

• GINGERED CARROT SOUP

1 onion
4 medium carrots
25 g butter
4 cups hot chicken stock

¼ teaspoon grated root ginger
Freshly ground black pepper
Salt
Sugar

Peel and roughly chop the onion and carrots. In a large microwave dish melt the butter on 70% power for 30 seconds. Add the onion and carrot stirring to coat the vegetables in butter. Cover and cook on High power (100%) for 5 minutes. Combine chicken stock and ginger. Purée carrot and stock mixtures in a blender. Return the soup to the dish. Microwave on High for 3 to 4 minutes to heat the soup through, stirring halfway through cooking. Season to taste with salt, pepper and sugar.
Serves 4 to 6.

• ITALIAN MUSSEL SOUP

12 live mussels
1 onion
¼ cup dry white wine

1½ cups tomato juice
Salt
Freshly ground black pepper

Scrub the mussels thoroughly with a brush, remove the beards and any tufts. Drain well. Peel and finely chop the onion. Put the onion and wine in a large microwave dish. Place the mussels in the dish. Cover, leaving a small steam vent. Microwave on High power (100%) for 4 to 6 minutes until the mussel shells have opened. Discard any mussels that do not open. Reserve half a cup of cooking liquid and the onion. Remove the mussels from the shells and cut into four. Return the reserved cooking liquid and onion to the microwave dish. Add the tomato juice, salt and pepper to the dish. Microwave on High for 3 minutes, stirring once during cooking. Remove from the microwave and stir in the chopped mussels. Serve immediately.
Serves 3 to 4.

SOUPS

• LEEK AND POTATO SOUP

1 large leek
2 cloves garlic
1 large potato
25 g butter

1 cup chicken stock
1 cup milk
¼ cup cream
Salt and pepper

Thinly slice the white part of the leek. Wash well. Crush, peel and mash the garlic. Peel and dice the potato. Put the butter in a microwave dish. Cover and microwave on High power (100%) for 30 seconds or until melted. Add leek, garlic and potato. Stir to coat the vegetables with butter. Cover. Microwave on High for 5 minutes or until vegetables are tender. Add chicken stock. Process in a food processor or blender until finely chopped. Return to the microwave. Add the milk. Microwave on High for 2 minutes, or until heated through. Add the cream and salt and pepper to taste.
Serves 2 to 3.

• LEMON AND BROCCOLI SOUP

500 g broccoli
2 tablespoons water
1 onion
1 small clove garlic
25 g butter
1 tablespoon flour

2 cups milk
¼ teaspoon dry mustard
1 to 2 tablespoons lemon juice
Salt
Freshly ground black pepper

Break broccoli into florets. Peel tough outer layer from stalks of broccoli. Dice the stalks. Put the florets and broccoli stalks into a microwave bowl. Add the water. Cover. Microwave on High power (100%) for 4 minutes or until tender. Set aside. Peel and chop the onion. Crush, peel and mash the garlic. Put the onion, garlic and butter into a glass microwave measuring jug. Microwave on High for 2 minutes or until onion is soft. Stir in the flour. Microwave on High for a further 1 minute. Gradually add the milk. Microwave on High for 3 minutes or until thick, stirring after 2 minutes. Combine broccoli and sauce. Process in a food processor until smooth. Return to microwave jug. Add mustard. Microwave on High for a further 2 minutes or until heated through. Stir in the lemon juice, salt and pepper. Serve hot.
Serves 4.

• LETTUCE SOUP

1 onion
6 large lettuce leaves
25 g butter
2 tablespoons flour
1¼ cups boiling chicken stock

1¼ cups milk .
¼ teaspoon sugar
Freshly ground black pepper
Pinch ground nutmeg
Salt

Peel and finely chop the onion. Wash and roughly chop the lettuce. Put the onion and butter into a microwave bowl. Microwave on High power (100%) for 2 minutes or until soft. Add lettuce, cook for a further 2 minutes. Stir in the flour. Microwave on High for 1 minute. Add chicken stock stirring to combine. Microwave on High for about 2 minutes, or until mixture thickens and boils. Purée in a blender or food processor. Stir in the milk. Microwave on High for a further 2 minutes. Season with sugar, pepper, nutmeg and salt. Serve garnished with shredded lettuce if wished. Serve hot or cold.
Serves 2-3.
NOTE: If serving chilled, ensure soup is very cold.

• MACARONI SOUP

2 onions
1 clove garlic
1 stalk celery
1 carrot
1 tablespoon oil
400 g can whole tomatoes in juice
¼ cup tomato purée

½ cup elbow macaroni
1½ cups boiling water
Salt
¼ teaspoon freshly ground black pepper
1 tablespoon chopped parsley

Peel and finely chop the onions. Crush, peel and mash the garlic. Trim and finely chop the celery. Scrub and finely chop the carrot. Place the vegetables in a 2 litre glass microwave jug. Stir in the oil. Microwave on High power (100%) for 3 minutes. Add the tomatoes and juice, tomato purée, macaroni and water. Break up the tomatoes. Cover and microwave on High for 10 minutes, stirring the soup twice during cooking time. Season with salt and pepper. Fold the parsley through the soup. Cover and stand 5 minutes before serving.
Serves 4.

• MILD CURRY CHICKEN AND ALPHABET SOUP

1 onion
1 clove garlic
1 teaspoon curry powder
25 g butter
1 teaspoon flour
3 cups boiling chicken stock

¼ cup Diamond alphabet pasta
1 cup cooked chicken
¼ teaspoon sugar
Salt
Freshly ground black pepper

Peel and finely chop the onion. Crush, peel and mash the garlic. Put the onion, garlic, curry powder and butter into a two-litre glass microwave measuring jug. Cover. Microwave on High power (100%) for 2 minutes, or until onion is soft. Stir in the flour, chicken stock and alphabet pasta. Microwave on High for 5 minutes, stirring twice during cooking time. Add chicken, sugar, salt and pepper. Serve hot.
Serves 3 to 4.

• PUMPKIN SOUP

500 g pumpkin
1 onion
100 g bacon

1 tablespoon butter
3 cups boiling chicken stock
Pepper

GARNISH:

1 tablespoon sour cream
1 teaspoon chopped chives

Deseed and peel the pumpkin. Cut the pumpkin flesh into 3cm slices. Peel and finely chop the onion. Remove rind from the bacon and roughly chop flesh. In a microwave container melt the butter on 50% power for 40 seconds. Add the onion and bacon. Cook on High power (100%) for 2 minutes. Add the pumpkin, cover and cook on High for 5 minutes or until cooked. Put the pumpkin, bacon, onion and chicken stock in a blender. Blend until smooth. Season with pepper. Pour into a serving bowl, garnish with sour cream and chives.
Serves 4 to 5.

The flavour of microwave soups develops if left to stand so ideally it is better to make them the day before.

SOUPS

• PEA AND HAM SOUP

½ cup yellow split peas
1 cup boiling water
1 large onion
1 cup boiling water
1 tablespoon butter

1 tablespoon flour
1 cooked bacon hock
Salt
Freshly ground black pepper

Put split peas and first measure of water into a bowl. Leave to soak 1 hour. Peel and roughly chop the onion. Transfer undrained pea mixture and second measure of water to a microwave bowl or measuring jug with the onion. Cover. Microwave on 70% power for 20 minutes or until peas are tender. Process in a food processor until smooth. Put the butter in a microwave bowl. Cover. Microwave on High power (100%) for 1 minute. Stir in the flour and puréed pea mixture. Remove and chop the flesh from bacon hock. Add to peas. Microwave on High for 3 minutes or until heated through and thickened. Season with salt and pepper.
Serves 4.

To Cook The Bacon Hock:

Place hock with quarter of a cup of boiling water in a microwave bowl. Microwave on High power (100%) for 30 seconds then microwave for 15 minutes on 70% power or until flesh is tender.

• QUICK ASPARAGUS SOUP

1 onion
1 tablespoon butter
1 tablespoon flour
340 g can asparagus spears

1½ cups milk
½ cup reserved asparagus brine
½ cup grated cheese
Freshly ground black pepper

Peel and chop the onion. Put the onion and butter in a microwave jug. Microwave on High power (100%) for 1 minute. Stir in the flour and microwave on high for a further minute. Drain the asparagus, reserving half a cup of brine. Combine the reserved brine and milk. Stir the milk mixture into the flour mixture. Microwave on High for 3 minutes or until sauce thickens and boils, stirring after 1 minute. Stir in the cheese. Process the asparagus in a food processor or blender until minced. Combine sauce with asparagus. Season to taste with pepper. Serve immediately.
Serves 4.

• SMOKED FISH CHOWDER

1 cup diced raw potato
½ cup finely chopped onion
½ cup diced celery
25 g butter
1½ tablespoons flour
2 cups milk

½ cup grated cheese
1 cup boiling water
1½ cups flaked smoked fish
Salt
Freshly ground black pepper
¼ cup finely chopped parsley

In a two-litre glass microwave measuring jug put the potato, onion, celery and butter. Microwave on High power (100%) for 3 minutes, or until vegetables are soft, stirring after 1 minute. Add flour, mix to combine. Cook for a further 1 minute. Stir in the milk. Microwave on High for a further 3 minutes, or until sauce thickens and boils, stirring after 2 minutes. Add grated cheese, water and smoked fish. Microwave on High for 1 minute. Season with salt and pepper. Serve garnished with parsley.
Serves 4 to 5.

• SILVERBEET AND CORN SOUP

8 silverbeet leaves
3 tablespoons Fielders cornflour
600 ml milk
1 teaspoon chicken stock powder

310 g can whole kernel corn
1 cup grated cheese
Freshly ground black pepper

Wash silverbeet, slit down centre of stems and chop. Place in a large microwave bowl, cover and microwave on High power (100%) for 2 minutes. Blend cornflour with some of the milk. Add to the silverbeet with remaining milk and chicken stock, stir. Microwave on High for about 8 minutes, until mixture boils and thickens. Stir after 4 minutes. Add drained corn and microwave on High for 1 minute. Stir in cheese and black pepper.
Serves 4.

• SWEETCORN CHOWDER

2 rashers bacon
1 large onion
1 potato
¼ cup finely chopped green pepper
25 g butter

1½ tablespoons flour
2 cups boiling chicken stock
450 g can sweetcorn kernels
1½ cups milk

Derind and roughly chop the bacon. Peel and finely chop the onion. Peel and dice the potato. Put the bacon, onion, potato, pepper and butter into a two-litre microwave measuring jug. Cover. Microwave on High power (100%) for 3 minutes or until vegetables are soft. Stir in the flour. Microwave on High for 1 minute. Gradually add the chicken stock, stirring all the time. Drain the sweetcorn and add to the vegetable mixture. Return to the microwave and cook on High for 10 minutes. Mash slightly. Stir in the milk.
Serves 6 to 8.

• VEGETABLE SOUP

350 g pumpkin
1 potato

¼-½ cup water
1 leek

Deseed pumpkin and cut into large serving sized pieces. Wash the potato and cut into quarters. Place pumpkin in the centre of a round microwave dish. Arrange the potato pieces near the edge of the dish. Pour quarter to half a cup of water over the vegetables. Cover and microwave on High power (100%) for 7 to 8 minutes. Leave to stand for 2 minutes. Remove lid and allow vegetables to cool. Remove pumpkin and potato skins and cut vegetables into small bite-sized pieces. Trim leek and split in half lengthwise, cutting only to the centre. Rinse under cold water and finely slice the leek. Place leeks into a covered dish and microwave on High for 4 to 5 minutes. Stand for 1 minute. Mix the sauce with the vegetable pieces. Fold gently to avoid breaking the potato and pumpkin. Reheat for 2 minutes on High.
Serves 4.

SAUCE:

2 tablespoons butter
2 tablespoons flour
1 cup milk

1 cup chicken stock
White pepper

Melt butter on High power (100%) for 1 minute. Add flour, milk and chicken stock. Season with pepper. Beat well. Cook on High for 4 minutes. Stir to mix.

• BACON AND EGG MOUSETRAPS

2 slices toast cut bread
2 eggs

1 teaspoon bacon stock powder
About 1 cup grated cheese

Toast bread, place on a plate and press over surface of toast so the crusts form sides to hold the eggs. Break eggs on top and pierce yolks and whites. Sprinkle half the bacon stock powder over each piece then sprinkle with cheese. Microwave on High (100%) 1-1½ minutes.

• CAULIFLOWER CHEESE

1 small cauliflower, about 500g in weight
Toasted breadcrumbs

Trim cauliflower and cut into florets, then cut slits in bottom of stalks. Rinse under cold water. Tightly pack the cauliflower into a glass microwave jug or casserole dish. Cook on High power (100%) for about 6 to 8 minutes or until just cooked. Leave to stand 3 minutes. Combine sauce and cauliflower. Top with breadcrumbs.
Serves 3 to 4.

CHEESE SAUCE:

1 onion
2 tablespoons butter
2 tablespoons flour
2 cups milk

Salt
White pepper
½ to ¾ cup grated cheese
½ teaspoon prepared mustard

Peel and chop the onion. Put the butter and onion into a microwave jug. Microwave on High power (100%) for about 1 minute. Stir in the flour. Microwave for a further minute. Stir in the milk. Return to the microwave and cook on High for about 3 minutes or until sauce thickens, stirring twice during cooking time. Stir in the salt, pepper, cheese and mustard.

• CHEESE AND BACON SPREAD

3 rashers bacon
25 g butter
2 cups grated tasty cheese
Pinch cayenne pepper
2 eggs

½ cup cream or milk
Freshly ground black pepper
Parsley for garnish
Crackers or melba toast

Remove rind from the bacon. Place rashers between two paper towels. Microwave on High power (100%) for 3 to 4 minutes or until bacon is cooked. Dice the bacon. Put the butter and cheese into a microwave bowl. Microwave on 70% power for 2 minutes or until melted. Add cayenne pepper. Beat eggs and cream together. Gradually mix into the melted cheese. Microwave on 70% power for about 4 minutes, stirring every minute until mixture is thick and smooth. Add bacon and pepper to taste. Pour into a ramekin dish. Refrigerate until firm. Garnish with parsley. Serve with crackers or melba toast.

For foods that have thick and thin ends such as some fish, broccoli and chicken pieces, place the thickest part to the outside of the dish.

• CHEESE SOUFFLÉ

2 spring onions
50g butter
2 tablespoons flour
1 cup milk
¼ teaspoon dry mustard

Salt
Freshly ground black pepper
3 eggs
¾ cup grated tasty cheese
Paprika

Finely chop the spring onions. Put the spring onions and butter into a one-litre glass microwave jug. Cover and microwave on High (100%) for 1 minute. Add the flour, stir to combine. Microwave on High for 1 minute. Gradually add the milk stirring all the time. Microwave on High for 3 minutes or until thick, stirring every minute. Add mustard, salt and pepper. Leave to cool slightly. Separate the eggs. Beat the egg yolks into the sauce. Add all but one tablespoon of the cheese to the sauce, stir to combine. Beat egg whites until stiff. Fold egg whites into sauce mixture. Lightly grease a 5 cup capacity glass soufflé dish. Pour mixture into prepared dish, smoothing over the top. Sprinkle with reserved cheese. Set on a trivet. Microwave on 30% power for 10 minutes or until soufflé has risen. Sprinkle with a little paprika.
Serves 4.

• CHICKEN QUICHE

BASE:

1 cup long grain rice
2 tablespoons chicken stock powder

2¼ cups boiling water
1 egg

FILLING:

1 onion
1 tablespoon butter
1½ tablespoons flour
½ cup chicken stock
¼ cup milk

1½ cups cooked chicken
Freshly ground black pepper
2 eggs
¾ cup grated cheese
1 tablespoon parsley

BASE:

Combine the rice, stock powder and water in a two-litre glass microwave jug. Cover and cook on High power (100%) for 12 minutes. Leave to stand 5 minutes. Beat in the egg. Line a 23cm microwave quiche dish with the rice mixture covering base and sides. Spoon filling into rice shell. Microwave on High for 10 minutes. Stand 5 minutes.
Serves 6 to 8.

FILLING:

Peel and finely chop the onion. Put onion and butter into a glass microwave jug. Cook on High power (100%) for 1 minute. Stir in the flour, cook for a further minute. Add chicken stock and milk. Microwave on High for 2 minutes. Stir in the chicken and microwave on High for a further 2 minutes. Add pepper. Lightly beat the eggs and add to sauce with the cheese and parsley.

If cooking uneven meats cover the thinner parts with foil part way through cooking to prevent further cooking.

LIGHT MEALS

• CHICKEN AND CORN TACOS

½ cooked boned chicken
1 small onion
1 small green pepper
2 tomatoes

½ cup whole kernel sweetcorn
10 taco shells
Avocado slices
About 2 cups shredded lettuce

SAUCE:

2 to 3 spring onions
250 g pot sour cream
1 teaspoon chilli sauce
1 tablespoon tomato sauce

1 tablespoon lemon juice
Freshly ground black pepper
Salt

Roughly chop the chicken flesh. Peel and finely chop the onion. Deseed and finely chop the pepper. Halve and deseed the tomatoes, chop the flesh. In a microwave bowl combine the chicken, onion, pepper, tomatoes and sweetcorn. Cover and microwave on High power (100%) for 4 minutes or until hot. Add the sauce mixing to combine. Divide the mixture evenly among the taco shells. Place two avocado slices on top, then some shredded lettuce.

SAUCE:

Finely chop the spring onions. Combine spring onions, sour cream, chilli sauce, tomato sauce, lemon juice, salt and pepper.

• CORNISH PUDDING

1 clove garlic
1 tablespoon butter
6 slices sandwich bread
3 slices ham
Paprika

4 eggs
1½ tablespoons flour
¾ cup milk
1 cup grated cheese
2 teaspoons chopped parsley

Crush, peel and mash the garlic. Put the garlic and butter into a small microwave dish. Cover with microwave-safe plastic wrap. Microwave on High power (100%) for 20 seconds. Mix to combine. Spread the slices of bread with garlic butter. Sandwich the ham between the slices of bread making three full sandwiches. Spread remaining garlic mixture on top surface of each sandwich. Sprinkle with paprika. Cut each sandwich into four on the diagonal. Arrange cut sandwiches in a 22cm shallow flan dish. In a one-litre glass microwave jug beat the eggs and flour together. Add milk, mix to combine. Microwave on 70% power for about 3 minutes or until mixture is hot and thickens slightly. Stir frequently during cooking time. Do not allow to boil. Leave to cool slightly. Add the cheese to the egg mixture. Pour mixture over the sandwiches. Press the bread into custard. Leave to stand 10 minutes or until the bread has soaked up most of the custard. Sprinkle with chopped parsley. Cover with microwave-safe plastic wrap. Elevate and microwave on 50% power for 8 to 10 minutes or until set. Serve hot.
Serves 4 to 5.

• CURRIED CHICKEN LIVERS ON TOAST

3 spring onions	2 teaspoons tomato chutney
1 clove garlic	1 teaspoon chicken stock powder
100 g chicken livers	¼ cup water
2 teaspoons butter	Freshly ground black pepper
1 teaspoon Indian curry powder	2 to 3 slices of toast

Trim and finely slice the spring onions. Crush, peel and mash the garlic. Drain and slice the chicken livers. Put the butter, spring onions, garlic and curry powder into a microwave bowl or measuring jug. Microwave on High power (100%) for 2 minutes. Add the chicken livers, chutney, stock powder, water and pepper. Cover and microwave on High for 3 minutes or until livers are just cooked. Stir once during cooking. Serve on toast.
Serves 2 to 3.

• EGG AND ASPARAGUS CASSEROLE

1 onion	½ cup reserved asparagus liquid
1 tablespoon butter	¾ cup grated tasty cheese
1 tablespoon flour	4 hard-boiled eggs
340 g can asparagus spears	2 tablespoons toasted breadcrumbs
½ cup milk	

Peel and finely chop the onion. Put the onion and butter into a one-litre glass microwave jug. Microwave on High power (100%) for 2 minutes. Stir in the flour, cook on High for 30 seconds. Carefully drain the asparagus spears reserving half a cup of the liquid. Combine the milk and reserved liquid. Gradually add the milk mixture to the measuring jug stirring to mix. Microwave on High for 4 minutes stirring after 2 minutes. Fold the cheese into the sauce. Place the asparagus spears in the base of a 20cm microwave dish. Shell the eggs and roughly chop. Spoon the chopped egg over the asparagus. Pour the sauce over the asparagus and egg. Microwave on High for 2 minutes. Sprinkle with breadcrumbs.
Serves 4.

• HOT DOGS

½ small onion	1 frankfurter
1 teaspoon butter	Tomato sauce
1 long bread roll	Prepared mustard

Peel and finely slice the onion. Put the butter and onion into a small microwave bowl or jug. Cover with microwave-safe plastic wrap. Microwave on High power (100%) for 1 minute. Cut the roll in half making the cut along the top of the roll, not the side. Carefully ease the roll open. Spoon onion into the bottom. Place frankfurter on top. Squeeze a little tomato sauce and mustard onto the frankfurter. Wrap in a paper towel. Microwave on High for about 45 seconds or until heated through. Do not overcook as roll will become chewy.
Serves 1.

◄ RICE Curried Rice Salad, Smoked Fish Kedgeree and Rice and Apricot Stuffed Cabbage Leaves.

LIGHT MEALS

• MUFFIN BURGERS

500 g topside mince
250 g sausage meat
31 g packet onion soup mix
2 tablespoons tomato sauce
1 teaspoon DYC soy sauce

4 English muffins
Tomato sauce
4 cheese slices
Tomato slices
¼ cup sliced gherkins

Put the mince into a mixing bowl. Add the sausage meat, soup mix, tomato sauce and soy sauce. Mix well to combine. Divide mixture into four. Shape into rounds. Heat a browning dish for 6 minutes. Place hamburger patties on hot dish. Cook on High power (100%) for 2 minutes then turn over and cook for a further 4 minutes or until meat is cooked. Do not overcook. Leave to stand while preparing muffin. Cut muffin in half and toast. Spread with a little tomato sauce. Top with hamburger pattie. Place a slice of cheese, tomato and gherkin on top. Place other half of muffin on top.
Serves 4.

• MUSHROOM SAVOURY

250 g button mushrooms
4 rashers bacon
3 spring onions
2 cloves garlic
25 g butter
2 tablespoons Fielders cornflour

1½ cups milk
Salt
Freshly ground black pepper
2 tablespoons cream or top of milk
1 tablespoon parsley

Wipe and slice the mushrooms. Derind and finely chop the bacon. Finely chop the spring onions. Crush, peel and mash the garlic. Put the butter, bacon, onion and garlic into a two-litre glass microwave measuring jug. Cover and microwave on High power (100%) for about 4 minutes or until cooked. Gradually mix the cornflour and milk to a smooth paste. Add to the jug. Season with salt and pepper. Add the mushrooms. Return to the microwave and microwave on High power for a further 8 to 10 minutes or until sauce thickens, stirring every 2 minutes. Stir in the cream and parsley. Serve on a bed of rice.
Serves 2 to 3

• MUSHROOMS A LA GRECQUE

1 cup hot water
¼ cup lemon juice
1 bay leaf
6 black peppercorns

6 coriander seeds
250 g button mushrooms
¼ cup olive oil
Salt

Put the hot water, lemon juice, bay leaf, peppercorns and coriander seeds into a microwave bowl. Microwave on High power (100%) for 5 minutes or until almost boiling. Wipe the mushrooms and add to bowl. Microwave on High for a further 1½ minutes. Add the oil. Leave until cool then refrigerate until cold. Season with salt before serving.
Serves 4

Only use plastics designed for microwave use. Many plastics contain impurities and cannot be used safely in the microwave.

• PARSLEY AND BACON POTATO BAKE

3 rashers bacon
¾ teaspoon salt
¼ cup finely chopped parsley
2 tablespoons flour
Freshly ground black pepper

4 large potatoes
50g butter
1 cup evaporated milk
1 cup grated cheese

Derind the bacon. Put the rashers between two paper towels. Place on a plate. Cook on High power (100%) for 2 to 2½ minutes or until the fat begins to colour. Finely chop flesh. Mix the bacon, salt, parsley, flour and pepper together. Peel and finely slice the potatoes. Layer a third of the potatoes in a six-cup capacity microwave dish. Sprinkle over half the bacon mixture. Repeat the layers finishing with a layer of potatoes. Dot with the butter. Pour over the milk. Place on a microwave rack in the microwave and cook on High for 14 to 15 minutes or until the potatoes are tender. Top the potatoes with the cheese and brown under a hot grill.
Serves 5 to 6.

• PIZZA

BASE:
1 cup flour
½ teaspoon salt
1 teaspoon DYC dried yeast
¼ teaspoon sugar

About 2 cups lukewarm milk
2 teaspoons oil
½ cup grated tasty cheese
or mozzarella

TOMATO TOPPING:
2 cloves garlic
¼ cup tomato purée

¼ teaspoon oregano

TOPPING SUGGESTIONS:
Ham and pineapple
Salami and tomato
Tuna, olives and anchovies
Asparagus and mushrooms

Ham, red and green peppers
Grated courgettes, mushrooms
and peppers

Sift flour and salt into a mixing bowl. Sprinkle yeast and sugar over the milk. Set aside until frothy. Make a well in the centre of the flour. Pour yeast mixture into the well. Add the oil. Gradually mix the flour into the yeast mixture until combined. Knead until a soft pliable dough is formed. Place in a microwave bowl. Cover and microwave on 30% power for 1 minute. Leave to stand 10 minutes. Repeat until dough has doubled in bulk. Punch down and lightly knead. Roll into a 25cm round. Carefully lift onto a 25cm microwave plate. Spread with tomato topping and sprinkle with cheese. Then arrange any topping combination on top. Microwave on High power (100%) for 5 to 6 minutes or until base is cooked. Quickly transfer the pizza to a serving plate.
Serves 4 to 5.

TOMATO TOPPING:

Crush, peel and mash the garlic. Combine garlic, tomato purée and oregano.

If browning dish is available, heat browning dish on High for 6 minutes. Place complete pizza onto base and microwave on High for 5 to 6 minutes or until cooked.

The denser the texture of a food the longer the cooking process carries on after food is taken from the oven.

LIGHT MEALS

• PIZZA OMELET

1 small potato	1 clove garlic
1 courgette	1 tablespoon butter
½ green pepper	3 eggs
4 button mushrooms	1 tablespoon chopped fresh chives

Peel and dice the potato. Wash and grate the courgette. Finely chop the pepper. Wipe and slice the mushrooms. Crush, peel and mash the garlic. Combine the vegetables. Put the butter in a shallow 20cm microwave pie plate. Cover and microwave on High power (100%) for about 40 seconds or until melted. Add the vegetables stirring to coat the vegetables with butter. Cover and microwave on High for 6 minutes stirring occasionally. Lightly beat the eggs. Stir eggs into the vegetable mixture. Sprinkle with chives. Cover and cook on 70% power for 3 minutes or until just set. Leave to stand 1 minute before serving.
Serves 2 to 3.

• POTATO AND TUNA BAKE

1 large potato	Freshly ground black pepper
1 tablespoon water	¼ cup cream
310 g can asparagus spears	¼ cup mayonnaise
340 g can tuna	1 tablespoon grated parmesan cheese
1 small onion	Chopped chives for garnish
¼ cup chopped green pepper	

Peel and thinly slice the potato. Wash under cold water. Arrange potato slices over the base of a shallow microwave dish. Sprinkle with the water. Cover and microwave on High power (100%) for about 5 minutes or until potato is tender. Drain. Drain the asparagus. Arrange over the potatoes. Drain the tuna. Peel and finely chop the onion. Combine the tuna, onion and green pepper. Season with pepper. Spoon the tuna mixture over the asparagus. Combine cream and mayonnaise. Spoon mixture on top. Sprinkle with parmesan cheese. Cover with vented microwave-safe plastic wrap. Microwave on High for 3 minutes or until heated through. Garnish with chopped chives.
Serves 2 to 3.

• PUMPKIN AND HAM CASSEROLE

About 375 g butternut pumpkin	Freshly ground black pepper
1 ham steak	½ cup cream or milk
½ cup finely chopped spring onions	Paprika
1 cup grated cheese	

Remove seeds and skin from pumpkin. Thinly slice the flesh. Arrange half the pumpkin on the base of a shallow microwave dish. Dice the ham steak. Spoon half the ham, spring onion and cheese on top. Repeat with remaining pumpkin, ham and cheese. Season with pepper. Pour cream on top. Elevate and cook on High power (100%) for about 10 minutes or until tender. Garnish with paprika.
Serves 2 to 3.

Pre-cook any hard vegetables that may be included in casseroles.

• QUICK LUNCHEON PIZZAS

4 pita bread
About 2 tablespoons prepared
    pizza sauce

½ cup grated tasty cheese
½ cup chopped ham
2 tablespoons crushed pineapple

Spread each pita bread with pizza sauce. Top with grated cheese. Sprinkle the ham and pineapple over the cheese. Place the pita pizza on a paper towel. Microwave on High power (100%) for 2 minutes, or until cheese has melted. Makes 4.

• SALAMI SNACKS

1 loaf French bread
Butter
1 onion

About 1 tablespoon chilli sauce
12 slices salami
About ½ cup grated cheese

Cut the French bread into three even-sized pieces. Cut each piece in half horizontally. Butter each piece of bread. Peel and finely chop the onion. Spread each piece of bread with a little chilli sauce then sprinkle with onion. Top with two pieces of salami. Sprinkle with grated cheese. Microwave each piece on High power (100%) for 40 seconds or until cheese melts and bread is heated through.
Makes 6.

• SALMON AND CHEESE RING

3 eggs
1 cup milk
2 tablespoons dry white wine
1 tablespoon chopped parsley
1 teaspoon chopped fresh dill
1 tablespoon lemon juice

Freshly ground black pepper
4 slices toast bread
½ cup grated cheese
213 g can salmon
2 tablespoons reserved salmon brine

In a one-litre glass microwave jug combine eggs, milk, wine, parsley, dill, lemon juice and pepper. Microwave on 70% power for 4 to 5 minutes or until mixture is hot and starting to thicken. Do not allow to boil. Stir frequently during cooking time, Cut the bread into cubes. Add bread and cheese to egg mixture. Drain and flake the salmon reserving two tablespoons of brine. Add salmon and brine to egg mixture. Mix to combine. Spoon mixture into a 22cm glass microwave ring mould. Cover with a paper towel. Microwave on 50% power for 8 to 10 minutes or until centre is almost set. Leave to stand 5 minutes before turning out. Serve hot or cold.
Serves 6.

When using the microwave for casseroles ensure all meat to be cooked is immersed in the liquid. If not, sit a plate on top to correct the problem. Use less liquid in casseroles than you would in conventional cooking.

LIGHT MEALS

• SCOTCH EGGS

500 g sausage meat
¼ cup finely chopped onion
1 tablespoon tomato sauce
1 teaspoon DYC soy sauce

1 tablespoon chopped parsley
4 hard-boiled eggs
About ¾ cup toasted breadcrumbs

Put the sausage meat into a mixing bowl. Add the onion, tomato sauce, soy sauce and parsley. Mix well to combine. Divide mixture evenly into four portions. Shell the eggs. With wet hands form the mixture around each egg. Roll in crumbs. Microwave each egg on High power (100%) for about 2 minutes or until sausage meat is firm. Turn after 1 minute to cook evenly. Allow to cool slightly before halving and serving.
Makes 4.

• SCRAMBLED EGGS

1 tablespoon butter
4 eggs

¼ cup milk
Salt and pepper

Melt butter in a 20 cm round dish on High power (100%). Whisk in eggs, milk and seasonings. Cover and cook on 70% power for 3 - 4 minutes, pushing cooked egg to the middle after 2 minutes. Stir and stand 1½ minutes. For variety add grated cheese, chopped chives, minced onion, parsley, herbs etc during the first stir.

• SMOKED FISH CHARLOTTE

1 onion
1 tablespoon butter
1 tablespoon Fielders cornflour
1 cup milk

2 eggs
310 g can smoked fish fillets
Freshly ground black pepper
2 teaspoons chopped parsley

SAVOURY TOASTED BREAD:

2 tablespoons butter
¼ teaspoon garlic salt

½ teaspoon curry powder
4 slices sandwich bread

Peel and finely chop the onion. Put the onion and butter into a two-litre glass microwave measuring jug. Microwave on High power (100%) for 2 minutes. Gradually combine the cornflour and milk until smooth. Microwave on High for 4 minutes, stirring frequently. Lightly beat the eggs. Add to the sauce. Drain and flake the fish. Combine the sauce and fish. Return to microwave and cook on High for a further 2 minutes or until mixture is hot, stir after 1 minute. Spoon mixture into a shallow serving casserole dish. Arrange the savoury toasted bread on top. Garnish with chopped parsley. Serve hot.
Serves 4.

SAVOURY TOASTED BREAD:

Combine butter, garlic salt and curry powder. Microwave on High power (100%) for 25 seconds or until soft. Spread mixture onto slices of bread. Cut slices into four on the diagonal. Arrange on a ridged microwave dish or paper towels. Microwave on High for about 1 minute or until crisp.

Always choose a time option that undercooks the food cooked in the microwave. It is simple to add time to complete cooking.

• STUFFED AVOCADO

2 ripe avocados

Cut avocados in half lengthwise. Remove stone. Spoon shrimp mixture into stone cavity. Place on a glass microwave dish, narrow ends towards the centre. Microwave on 50% power for about 2 minutes or until filling is just heated through.
Serves 4.

FILLING:

200 g can shrimps	2 teaspoons chopped parsley
½ cup mayonnaise	¼ teaspoon grated lemon rind
1 tablespoon chopped chives	Freshly ground black pepper

Drain and wash the shrimps. Drain well. Combine the mayonnaise, chives, parsley and lemon rind. Stir in the shrimps. Season with pepper to taste. Use to fill the avocados.

• STUFFED CRÊPES

BATTER:

½ cup flour	About ¾ cup milk
¼ teaspoon salt	1 teaspoon melted butter
1 egg	

Sift the flour and salt into a bowl. Beat the egg and add the milk, mix to combine. Gradually add the egg mixture to the flour mixing to form a smooth paste. Continue adding the liquid until a smooth batter is formed. Put into a jug and refrigerate for about 30 minutes. Add the melted butter. Lightly grease a pancake pan or small frying pan. Heat the pan. Stir batter twice after standing. Pour a little batter into the pan, rotating the pan so the batter evenly and thinly coats the base of the pan. Cook the pancake until the underneath is golden brown, then toss to cook the other side. Repeat until all the batter is used. Stack the pancakes on top of each other until ready to use. Spoon filling evenly among the pancakes. Arrange the pancakes onto a shallow dish. Cover with vented microwave-safe plastic wrap and microwave on High power (100%) for about 4 minutes or until filling is heated through.
Makes 6.

FILLING:

100 g button mushrooms	1 tablespoon lemon juice
1 small onion	Salt
25 g butter	Freshly ground black pepper
2 teaspoons flour	1 tablespoon chopped parsley
½ cup light cream or milk	4 hard-boiled eggs

Wipe and slice the mushrooms. Peel and finely chop the onion. Put the butter, mushrooms and onion in a microwave glass jug. Cover and microwave on High power (100%) for 2 minutes or until onion is clear. Stir in the flour. Microwave for a further minute. Gradually add the cream stirring all the time. Microwave on 70% power for 1 to 2 minutes or until sauce thickens. Stir in the lemon juice, salt, pepper and parsley. Shell the eggs then cut into quarters. Add the eggs to the sauce. Use to fill pancakes.

Always use microwave-safe plastic wrap for microwave cooking. This is marked on the box or wrapper.

LIGHT MEALS

• STUFFED JACKET POTATOES

2 medium even-sized potatoes
1 tablespoon butter

Salt
Freshly ground black pepper

FILLING SUGGESTIONS:

Grated cheese and celery
Grated cheese and onion
Grated cheese and chutney
Ham and pineapple

Tuna and mayonnaise
Creamed style sweet corn
Salami, tomato and cheese

Scrub potatoes then prick 4 to 5 times. Pack tightly into a microwave container. Microwave on High power (100%) for about 4 minutes. Turn the potatoes over and continue cooking for 3 to 4 minutes or until potatoes feel slightly soft but not cooked through. Leave to stand 2 minutes. Cut the top third of potato off. Scoop out the flesh from the potato and lid. Mash with butter and season with salt and pepper then add other filling ingredients. Scoop filling back into skins. Reheat on High for about 2 minutes or until filling is heated through.
Serves 2

• STUFFED PITA POCKETS

4 small pita bread rounds
¼ cup chopped spring onions
½ cup creamed style sweet corn

½ cup chopped salami
¼ cup grated tasty cheese

Cut a small horizontal slit in each bread. Gently open to form a pocket. Spoon a little of the spring onion, sweetcorn, salami and cheese into each pocket. Wrap pockets in a paper towel. Place pockets upright in a microwave container. Cook on High power (100%) for about 2 minutes or until heated through.
Makes 4.

• STUFFED TOMATOES

4 large tomatoes
About 1 cup cooked mince
½ cup grated cheese

½ teaspoon chopped fresh basil
Freshly ground black pepper

Wipe the tomatoes. Cut the tops off the tomatoes then carefully scoop out the pulp. Combine tomato pulp, mince and cheese. Spoon mixture into tomato shells. Place tomatoes into a shallow microwave casserole dish. Sprinkle with basil and pepper. Microwave on 70% power for 4 to 5 minutes or until filling is heated through.
Serves 4.

Cooking times will depend on the material of the cooking vessel. If you deviate from that specified in a recipe, the cooking time will probably differ.

• SWEETCORN AND BACON QUICHE

½ cup soft breadcrumbs
½ cup grated cheese
1 onion
3 rashers bacon
2 teaspoons oil

450g can creamed sweetcorn
3 eggs
½ cup milk
Salt
Freshly ground black pepper

Grease a 23cm microwave flan dish. Sprinkle the breadcrumbs over the base, pressing down slightly. Sprinkle the cheese over the base. Peel and finely chop the onion. Derind the bacon and cut the flesh into small pieces. Place the onion and bacon in a large glass microwave jug. Mix in the oil. Microwave on High power (100%) for 3 minutes. Add the sweetcorn to the bacon and onion mixture. Beat the eggs and milk together. Season with salt and pepper. Combine the egg and corn mixtures. Mix well. Spoon the filling into the dish. Microwave on High for 8 to 10 minutes or until the filling is almost completely set. Cover with a paper towel and stand 5 minutes. Serve warm.
Serves 6.

• WELSH RAREBIT

1 clove garlic
25 g butter
½ teaspoon dry mustard
1/8 teaspoon salt
Pinch cayenne pepper

Dash tabasco sauce
¾ cup grated tasty cheese
2 tablespoons milk
4 slices toast

Crush, peel and mash the garlic. In a microwave bowl combine the garlic and butter. Stir in the mustard, salt, cayenne pepper, tabasco, cheese and milk. Microwave on High power (100%) for about 30 seconds or until mixture is hot and bubbling. Beat until smooth. Spread on slices of toast. Place onto a microwave serving plate. Reheat on High for 20 seconds.
Serves 2.

• WHOLEMEAL MOUSIES

4 slices Vogels bread
Butter
About 2 tablespoons crunchy tomato
    relish

1 cup grated tasty cheese
¼ cup sliced spring onions
¼ cup chopped green pepper

Microwave the bread on High power (100%) for 4 minutes, Remove crusts and cut each slice in half. Spread with butter and relish. Sprinkle with cheese then top with spring onions and green pepper. Place bread on a paper towel. Microwave on High for a further 40 seconds or until cheese melts. Serve hot or cold.
Makes 8 pieces.

Prick foods with skins such as sausages, potatoes and tomatoes. This will help stop skins bursting and prevent the food exploding in the microwave.

• ALMOND AND RED PEPPER RICE

25 g butter
¼ cup sliced almonds
1 cup long grain rice

½ red pepper
½ teaspoon salt
1 ¾ cups water

Melt butter on High power (100%) for about 30 seconds, add almonds and cook on High for 2 to 3 minutes or until butter and almonds are browned, stirring occasionally. Set aside. Wash rice well and drain thoroughly. Remove seeds from pepper and dice. Combine rice, pepper, salt and water and cover with a paper towel. Cook on High for 14 minutes without stirring, or until all liquid has been absorbed. Leave covered 5 minutes then fluff up with a fork. Add almonds and butter and toss lightly.
Serves 4.

• CHICKEN PAELLA

150 g boned and skinned chicken
150 g lean pork
1 small onion
2 cloves garlic
1 tablespoon clarified butter
150 g garlic sausage or bier sticks

1 green or red pepper
2 tomatoes
1 cup long grain rice
1 ½ cups chicken stock
½ teaspoon turmeric
Salt and pepper

Cut chicken and pork into small cubes. Peel and chop onion and garlic. Preheat browning dish for maximum suggested time, add butter and swirl to coat dish. Quickly add chicken, pork, onion and garlic and toss well to brown all sides. Cook on High power (100%) for 2 minutes, stirring once. Skin garlic sausage and dice or cut into rounds. Remove seeds and slice pepper. Peel and chop tomatoes. Wash rice well. Transfer browned meat to large microwave dish. Add garlic sausage, pepper, tomatoes and rice. Stir in chicken stock, turmeric, salt and pepper. Cover closely with lid or plastic microwave-safe plastic wrap and cook on High without stirring for 15 minutes or until rice is tender.
Serves 4.

• CHICKEN, RICE AND APPLE SALAD

1 cup long grain rice
½ teaspoon salt
1 ¾ cups water
100 g skinned and boned chicken
1 tablespoon orange juice

1 cup frozen peas
1 red skinned apple
¼ cup mayonnaise
¼ cup natural unsweetened yoghurt
Salt and pepper

Wash rice well, drain thoroughly and combine with salt and water in a microwave bowl. Cover with a paper towel and cook on High power (100%) for 14 minutes without stirring, or until all liquid has been absorbed. Leave covered for 5 minutes then fluff up with a fork. Cool. Place chicken meat in a small microwave dish, tuck in any thin ends and pour over orange juice. Cover with a paper towel and cook on 70% power for 2 minutes or until just cooked. Cut into small cubes. Wash frozen peas in tepid water, drain and cook in a small covered container on High for about 3 minutes or until tender. Core apple and dice. Toss together rice, chicken, peas, mayonnaise, yoghurt, salt, pepper and diced apple. Chill well before serving.
Serves 4.

• CURRIED RICE SALAD

1 cup long grain rice
½ teaspoon salt
1¾ cups water
½ green pepper
½ red pepper
2 spring onions

2 tablespoons seedless raisins
2 tablespoons oil
2 tablespoons DYC vinegar
1 teaspoon curry powder
Salt and pepper
1 tablespoon lemon juice

Wash rice well, drain thoroughly and combine with salt and water in a microwave bowl. Cover with a paper towel and cook on High power (100%) for 14 minutes without stirring, or until all liquid has been absorbed. Leave covered for 5 minutes then fluff up with a fork. Cool. Remove seeds and dice green and red peppers. Slice spring onions finely. Add peppers, spring onions and raisins to cooled rice. Just before serving, shake together oil, vinegar, curry powder, salt, pepper and lemon juice. Sprinkle over rice mixture and toss with two forks.
Serves 4.

• FRIED RICE WITH HAM

1 cup long grain rice
½ teaspoon salt
1¾ cups water
2 eggs
1 small onion
1 clove garlic

3 cm piece root ginger
1 tablespoon olive oil
2 medium tomatoes
3 to 4 slices cooked ham
1 tablespoon DYC soy sauce
Salt and pepper

Wash rice well, drain thoroughly and combine with salt and water in a microwave bowl. Cook in microwave bowl on High power (100%) for 14 minutes without stirring, or until all liquid has been absorbed. Beat eggs and cook on stove top in a small frying pan until just set. Roll up and chop into thin strips. Peel and chop onion. Peel and finely chop garlic and ginger. Mix together oil, onion, garlic and ginger and cook in a large flat microwave dish on High for 1 to 2 minutes or until onion is soft. Peel and coarsely chop tomatoes. Slice ham. Add to onion mixture with tomatoes, sliced egg, cooked rice and soy sauce. Toss well and cook on High for about 5 minutes or until hot. Stir in salt and pepper before serving.
Serves 4.

• RICE AND COURGETTE LOAF

1 tablespoon butter
½ small onion
2 cloves garlic
3 courgettes
2 eggs

2 cups cooked rice
1 cup grated cheese
½ teaspoon ground nutmeg
Salt and pepper

Melt butter on High power (100%) for about 30 seconds. Peel and finely chop onion and garlic, add to butter and cook on High for 1½ minutes. Trim courgettes and grate. Beat eggs lightly. Mix rice, eggs, courgettes, butter and onion, cheese, nutmeg, salt and pepper. Turn into a lightly greased microwave loaf pan, smooth top. Protect ends from drying out with small strips of foil. Elevate and cook on 70% power for about 15 minutes or until firm.
Serves 4.

RICE

• RICE RING

50 g butter	3 cups cooked rice
1 small onion	½ teaspoon salt
2 eggs	¼ to ½ teaspoon chilli powder
150 g sliced ham	¼ cup finely chopped parsley

Melt butter on High power (100%) about 30 seconds or until just melted. Peel and chop onion, combine with butter and cook for 2 minutes. Separate eggs. Beat yolks. Dice ham. Stir together onion and butter, egg yolks, ham, cooked rice, salt, chilli powder and parsley. Beat egg whites to soft peaks and fold into mixture. Turn into a small lightly buttered microwave ring mould, smooth top. Elevate and cook on 70% power for 10 minutes.
Serve hot or cold.
Serves 4.

• RICE AND ADUKI BEAN CASSEROLE

2 medium carrots	3 tablespoons flour
2 stalks celery	1½ cups milk
1 cup brown rice	Salt and pepper
½ teaspoon salt	100 g blue vein cheese
1¾ cups water	2 cups cooked aduki beans
25 g butter	¼ cup chopped parsley

Peel carrots and cut in rings. Dice celery coarsely. Wash rice well, drain thoroughly and combine with carrots, celery, salt and water in a microwave bowl. Cover with a paper towel and cook on High power (100%) for 25 to 30 minutes without stirring, or until rice is soft. Melt butter on High for about 30 seconds in a microwave jug. Stir in flour and cook on High for 30 seconds. Gradually stir in milk making sure the ingredients are well blended together. Season with salt and pepper. Cook on High for 3 minutes, beating every minute until sauce has thickened. Crumble blue vein cheese and stir into sauce. Combine sauce with cooked rice and vegetables and aduki beans. Cook on 50% power for 10 minutes. Just before the end of cooking time stir in chopped parsley.
Serves 4.

• RICE AND APRICOT STUFFED CABBAGE LEAVES

8 cabbage leaves	1 cup cooked rice
6 dried apricots	Salt and pepper
½ cup water	¼ cup chopped parsley
½ small onion	1 red pepper
1 teaspoon oil	

Place cabbage leaves in a large microwave dish, cover and cook on High power (100%) for 3 minutes or until leaves begin to soften. Leave to cool. Cover apricots with water and cook on High for 2 minutes. Soak for about 5 minutes, drain and chop. Peel and finely chop onion. Mix with oil and cook on High for 1½ minutes. Stir in apricots, cooked rice, salt, pepper and chopped parsley. Cut central vein from cabbage leaves, lay out flat on bench and place equal quantities of rice mixture on each leaf. Fold up cabbage to form parcels. Arrange on a flat microwave dish. Remove seeds from red pepper and cut into rings. Place rings over and between cabbage parcels. Cover with microwave safe plastic wrap and cook on 70% power for about 10 minutes or until cabbage feels tender when tested with a knife.
Serves 4.

• RICE AND MINCE LOAF

1 small onion	1 teaspoon dried thyme
2 rashers bacon	1 egg
500 g topside mince	1 cup cooked rice
½ cup Flemings rolled oats	½ cup grated cheese
Salt and pepper	¼ cup fine toasted breadcrumbs

Peel and finely chop onion. Remove rind and chop bacon, mix with onion and cook on High power (100%) for 3 minutes. Stir in mince, rolled oats, salt, pepper and thyme. Separate egg, beat yolk and white separately. Mix egg white into mince mixture. Combine egg yolk with cooked rice and cheese. Cut a piece of greaseproof paper about 30 cm square and lay out on bench. Sprinkle with breadcrumbs. Turn out mince mixture and form into a 20cm square. Spread rice mixture over mince leaving a little room for spreading. Carefully roll up into a log shape. Place on a flat microwave dish and protect ends with thin strips of foil. Elevate and cook on 70% power for 12 to 15 minutes.
Serves 4.

• RICE AND MUSHROOM BAKE

1 cup long grain rice	1 cup soft breadcrumbs
½ teaspoon salt	1 cup grated cheese
1¾ cups water	1 teaspoon dried marjoram
200 g mushrooms	3 eggs
1 clove garlic	1 teaspoon paprika
25 g butter	

Wash rice well, drain thoroughly and combine with salt and water in a microwave dish. Cover with a paper towel and cook on High power (100%) for 14 minutes without stirring, or until all liquid has been absorbed. Leave covered 5 minutes then fluff up with a fork. Slice mushrooms. Crush and peel garlic. Melt butter on High for about 30 seconds. Add mushrooms and garlic and cook on High for 5 minutes. Use half of cooked rice to form a layer in the bottom of a medium-sized microwave dish. Spread over mushrooms then half of the measured breadcrumbs and cheese. Sprinkle over marjoram and add remaining rice, breadcrumbs and cheese. Beat eggs and pour over. Sprinkle with paprika. Elevate and cook on 50% power for 10 minutes.
Serves 4.

• RICE AND VEGETABLE PIE

1 cup long grain rice	1 medium onion
½ teaspoon salt	2 tablespoons oil
1¾ cups water	200 g broccoli
1 egg	200 g cauliflower
¾ cup grated cheese	½ cup grated cheese

Wash rice well, drain thoroughly and combine with salt and water in a microwave bowl. Cover with a paper towel and cook on High power (100%) for 14 minutes without stirring, or until all liquid has been absorbed. Leave covered 5 minutes then fluff up with a fork. Beat egg and mix into rice with first measure of cheese. Press into bottom and sides of a 25cm microwave flan dish. Peel and slice onion, stir in oil and cook on High for 2 minutes. Add broccoli and cauliflower. Cover and cook on High for 6 minutes, stirring once. Drain any liquid from vegetables before arranging over rice. Sprinkle with second measure of cheese. Elevate and cook on 50% power for about 10 minutes or until base is firm.
Serves 4.

RICE

• RICE STUFFED TOMATOES

4 to 6 large tomatoes	¼ cup grated tasty cheese
1 egg	¼ teaspoon chilli powder
1½ cups cooked rice	½ teaspoon paprika
2 tablespoons grated parmesan cheese	Salt and pepper

Slice top off tomatoes and carefully scoop out flesh. Use for another dish. Beat egg, add cooked rice, parmesan, tasty cheese, chilli powder, paprika, salt and pepper. Mix well and fill into tomato shells. Place in circle on flat microwave dish. Cook on 50% power for about 8 to 10 minutes, or until tomatoes are soft and filling has set.
Serves 4.

• SMOKED FISH KEDGEREE

1 cup long grain rice	300 g smoked fish
½ teaspoon salt	2 hard-boiled eggs
1¾ cups water	¼ cup chopped parsley
25 g butter	¼ teaspoon cayenne pepper
1 small onion	Black pepper

Wash rice well, drain thoroughly and combine with salt and water in a microwave bowl. Cover with a paper towel and cook on High power (100%) for 14 minutes without stirring, or until all liquid has been absorbed. Leave covered 5 minutes then fluff up with a fork. Melt butter on High for about 30 seconds. Peel and chop onion, add to butter and cook on High for 2 minutes. Place fish in a large flat dish, pour over hot water to cover and leave a few minutes to soften. Lift out and remove skin and bones from fish. Cut into small bite-sized pieces. Shell and slice hard-boiled eggs. Toss together cooked rice, butter and onion, smoked fish, sliced eggs, parsley, cayenne pepper and black pepper. Cover and cook on High for about 5 minutes or until piping hot.
Serves 4.

• SPINACH AND RICE STUFFED FILO PARCELS

1 bunch spinach	125 g cream cheese
50 g butter	1 teaspoon paprika
8 sheets filo pastry	Salt and pepper
1½ cups cooked rice	

Wash spinach and cut off stalks, place in covered dish with no extra water and cook on High power (100%) for 2 to 3 minutes. Drain and cool. Melt butter on High for about 45 seconds. Lay one sheet of filo pastry out on bench, brush with melted butter and cover with second layer of pastry. Chop spinach roughly, mix in rice. Warm cream cheese on 50% power for 1 minute. Stir into rice mixture with paprika, salt and pepper. Place a quarter of this mixture near shorter end of filo pastry. Fold up neatly to form a small parcel about 12cm x 7cm. Repeat these steps for remaining three parcels. Place on a flat lightly buttered microwave dish with pastry ends tucked underneath. Brush with remaining melted butter. Elevate and cook on High for 13 to 15 minutes. Pastry should be well puffed up but has no colour. Brown top surface slowly under preheated grill.
Serves 4.

Read your oven manual to check power level descriptions.

• VEGETABLE FRIED RICE

1 cup long grain rice
½ teaspoon salt
1¾ cups water
1 small onion
1 clove garlic
3 cm piece root ginger

1 tablespoon olive oil
1 small red pepper
2 small leaves silverbeet
425 g can baby corn
1 tablespoon DYC soy sauce
Salt and pepper

Wash rice well, drain thoroughly and combine with salt and water in a microwave bowl. Cover with a paper towel and cook on High power (100%) for 14 minutes without stirring, or until all liquid has been absorbed. Stand covered for 5 minutes then fluff up with a fork. Peel and chop onion. Peel and finely chop garlic and ginger. Mix together oil, onion, garlic and ginger and cook in a large flat microwave dish on High for 2 minutes. Remove seeds and cut red pepper into small dice. Add to onion and cook on High for 2 minutes. Cut white stem out of silverbeet and set aside for another recipe. Shred green of silverbeet finely. Drain baby corn. Add silverbeet, baby corn, soy sauce and cooked rice to onion and pepper mixture. Toss well and cook on High for 5 minutes or until silverbeet is just cooked. Season before serving.
Serves 4.

Every microwave oven is different. Treat cooking time given in a recipe as a guide NOT an absolute rule.

87

• BUTTERCUP STUFFED WITH SEASHELLS

150 g Diamond seashell pasta
1 teaspoon oil
1 tablespoon butter
1 medium carrot
½ cup frozen peas

1 egg
½ cup sliced almonds
½ teaspoon salt
1 large buttercup

Cook seashell pasta in boiling, salted water with oil for about 10 minutes, either in a saucepan or microwave on High power (100%) stirring halfway through cooking, until pasta is firm to the bite. Drain and rinse thoroughly. Cut up butter roughly. Peel and dice carrot. Mix together and cook covered for 2 minutes on High. Add peas and cook on High for 1 minute. Beat egg and stir into vegetables with sliced almonds, salt and cooked seashells. Wash buttercup well, slice off top and scoop out seeds. Fill cavity with pasta mixture, replace top to form a lid. Cook on a flat heatproof dish on High for 30 minutes.
Serves 4.

• COTTAGE CHEESE AND PASTA LOAF

1 medium onion
25 g butter
2 medium carrots
2 eggs
2 cups cooked Diamond spirals

250 g cottage cheese
1 teaspoon salt
¼ cup chopped parsley
1 tomato

Peel and finely chop onion. Chop butter roughly and cook with onion on High power (100%) for 2 minutes. Peel and grate carrots. Beat eggs lightly. Combine onion, carrots, eggs, spirals, cottage cheese, salt and parsley and mix well. Slice tomato thinly and use to decorate bottom of microwave loaf mould. Turn pasta mixture into mould, press down firmly and flatten top. Place strips of foil 8cm wide, over ends of loaf dish to prevent overcooking, elevate and cook on 70% power for about 18 minutes or until just firm to the touch. Serve cold.
Serves 4.

• HOT MACARONI SALAD

200 g Diamond macaroni elbows
1 teaspoon oil
1 medium onion
1 teaspoon butter
1 cup frozen peas
2 large gherkins

½ cup parsley
½ teaspoon salt
Pepper
3 tablespoons oil
3 tablespoons vinegar

Cook macaroni in boiling, salted water with oil for about 10 minutes, either in a saucepan or microwave on High power (100%), stirring halfway through cooking, until pasta is firm to the bite. Drain and rinse thoroughly. Peel and chop onion and cook with butter on High for 2 minutes. Wash peas in tepid water and cook on High in covered container for 2 to 3 minutes until just cooked. Drain. Slice gherkins and finely chop parsley. Carefully toss all ingredients together, cover with a paper towel and heat on High for 3 to 4 minutes. Toss lightly before serving.
Serves 4.

88

PASTA Buttercup Stuffed with Seashells, Lasagne and Vegetelli in an ▶
Egg Sauce.

• KLUSKI WITH TOMATOES

300 g Diamond kluski noodles
1 teaspoon oil
1 medium onion
1 teaspoon butter
1 medium green pepper

100 g mushrooms
425 g can peeled tomatoes in juice
1 teaspoon salt
Pepper

Cook kluski noodles in boiling, salted water with oil for about 10 minutes, either in a saucepan or microwave on High power (100%) for 8 to 10 minutes, stirring halfway through cooking, until pasta is firm to the bite. Drain and rinse thoroughly. Peel and chop onion and cook with butter on High for 3 minutes. Deseed and slice pepper, cut mushrooms into quarters and add pepper and mushrooms to onions. Cook on High for 2 minutes. Chop tomatoes coarsely and add with juice, salt and pepper to vegetable mixture. Cook on High for 5 minutes. Add cooked pasta, toss and cook on 70% power for 8 minutes. Serves 4.

• LASAGNE

300 g Diamond lasagne
1 teaspoon oil
1 medium onion
1 clove garlic
400 g minced steak
420 g can peeled tomatoes in juice
¼ cup tomato concentrate
1 teaspoon oregano

1 teaspoon salt
3 eggs
250 g cream cheese
½ cup grated tasty cheese
½ teaspoon salt
2 tablespoons grated parmesan
   cheese

Cook lasagne in boiling, salted water with oil for about 10 to 12 minutes, either in a saucepan or microwave on High power (100%) stirring halfway through cooking, until pasta is firm to the bite. Drain and rinse well. Meanwhile peel and chop onion and garlic, add broken up mince and cook on High for 4 minutes. Roughly chop tomatoes and add to mince with tomato concentrate, oregano and first measure of salt. Stir well and cook on High for 6 minutes. Beat eggs, mix in cream cheese, tasty cheese and second measure of salt. Use one-third of meat mixture to cover bottom of large rectangular microwave dish, lay over one-third of cooked lasagne and spoon over one-third of cheese mixture. Continue with layers of remaining ingredients in same order. Cover dish with lid or microwave-safe plastic wrap and cook on 70% power for 30 minutes. Sprinkle with parmesan cheese and brown under hot grill. Serves 4.

• LISCI WITH MUSHROOMS AND TUNA

300 g Diamond lisci
1 teaspoon oil
25 g butter
150 g button mushrooms
185 g can tuna

½ teaspoon salt
Freshly ground black pepper
150 ml cream
2 tablespoons finely chopped parsley

Cook lisci in boiling, salted water with oil for about 10 minutes, either in a saucepan or microwave on High power (100%), stirring halfway through, cooking until pasta is firm to the bite. Drain and rinse thoroughly. Melt butter on High for about 30 seconds. Halve mushrooms and add, toss well and cook on High for 3 minutes. Drain tuna, break into chunks. Toss lisci, mushrooms, tuna, salt, pepper, cream and parsley together and reheat on 70% power for about 4 minutes or until piping hot. Serves 4.

◀ FISH Fresh Mussels with Garlic and Wine. Tuna and Spinach Loaf and Fish Fillets with Vegetable Topping.

PASTA

• LUMACHE WITH SALAMI

300 g Diamond lumache pasta
1 teaspoon oil
1 medium onion
2 cloves garlic
1 tablespoon butter

250 g unsliced salami or smoked
   sausage
2 stalks celery
310 g can whole kernel corn
1 cup grated gruyere cheese

Cook lumache in boiling, salted water with oil for about 10 minutes, either in a saucepan or microwave on High power (100%) stirring halfway through cooking, until pasta is firm to the bite. Drain and rinse well. Peel and chop onion, peel and finely chop garlic. Chop butter roughly and mix with onion and garlic in large microwave container. Cook on High for 2 minutes. Cube salami or smoked sausage, dice celery and add with salami to onion. Stir and cook covered, on High for 3 minutes. Drain corn. Combine lumache, onion mixture, corn and cheese. Cook covered on 70% power for 6 minutes.
Serves 4.

• LUMACHE WITH THREE CHEESES

300 g Diamond lumache pasta
1 teaspoon oil
25 g butter
¼ cup grated parmesan cheese

50 g gruyere cheese
75g mozzarella cheese
Freshly ground black pepper

Cook lumache in boiling, salted water with oil for about 10 to 12 minutes, either in a saucepan or microwave on High power (100%) stirring halfway through cooking, until pasta is firm to the bite. Drain and rinse thoroughly. In the same large container, melt butter on High for about 30 seconds. Add cooked pasta and two-thirds of the parmesan cheese, toss well. Cut gruyere and mozzarella cheeses into small sticks about 2 to 3 cm long. Mix into pasta with black pepper. Transfer to serving dish and heat on 70% power for 4 to 5 minutes. Sprinkle with remaining parmesan cheese and place under hot grill to crisp and brown top.
Serves 4.

• MACARONI CHEESE

300 g Diamond macaroni elbows
1 teaspoon oil
2 rashers bacon
1 large onion

2 cloves garlic
2 tablespoons flour
2 cups milk
2 cups grated tasty cheese

Cook macaroni in boiling, salted water with oil for about 10 minutes, either in a saucepan or microwave on High power (100%) stirring halfway through cooking, until pasta is firm to the bite. Drain and rinse thoroughly. Remove rind from bacon and chop flesh coarsely. Peel and chop onion and garlic. Cook bacon, onion and garlic on High for 4 minutes. Stir in flour and cook on High for a further 1 minute. Blend in milk and cook on High for 5 minutes, stirring once. Mix in cheese and cooked macaroni and turn into microwave serving dish. Cook on 50% power for 10 to 15 minutes.
Serves 4.

• POPPY SEED NOODLES

250 g Diamond egg noodles
1 teaspoon oil
1 tablespoon butter
½ cup slivered almonds
3 tablespoons poppy seeds

1 teaspoon lemon juice
½ teaspoon salt
2 tablespoons finely chopped parsley
250 g sour cream

Cook egg noodles in boiling, salted water with oil for about 10 minutes, either in a saucepan or microwave on High power (100%), stirring halfway through cooking, until pasta is firm to the bite. Drain and rinse thoroughly. Melt butter on High for about 30 seconds, add almonds and toss well. Cook on High for 5 minutes to toast nuts, stirring occasionally. Stir all ingredients together well and heat on 70% power for about 5 minutes or until piping hot, stirring once. Serves 4.

• SPAGHETTI BOLOGNAISE

2 rashers bacon
1 onion
1 clove garlic
500 g minced steak
420 g can peeled tomatoes in juice
¼ cup tomato concentrate

¼ cup sherry
1 teaspoon oregano
½ teaspoon salt
300 g Diamond spaghetti
1 teaspoon oil
Grated parmesan cheese

Remove rind from bacon and chop flesh. Peel and chop onion and garlic. Combine with bacon and cook on High power (100%) for 4 minutes. Add mince, break up and cook on High for 4 minutes. Add tomatoes in juice, tomato concentrate, sherry, oregano and salt. Stir well and break up mince before cooking on High for 10 minutes. Cook spaghetti in boiling, salted water with oil for about 10 minutes, either in a saucepan or microwave on High, stirring halfway through cooking, until pasta is firm to the bite. Drain and rinse quickly with hot water. Arrange on serving plates, top with meat sauce and sprinkle with parmesan cheese.
Serves 4.

• SPAGHETTI MARINARA

300 g Diamond spaghetti
1 teaspoon oil
1 medium onion
2 cloves garlic
25 g butter
500 g tomatoes
1 teaspoon brown sugar

1 teaspoon oregano
1 teaspoon salt
6 cooked mussels
200 g can peeled prawns
25 g butter
¼ cup finely chopped parsley
Grated parmesan cheese

Cook spaghetti in boiling, salted water with oil for about 10 minutes, either in a saucepan or microwave on High power (100%) stirring halfway through cooking, until pasta is firm to the bite. Drain, rinse and keep hot. Meanwhile peel and chop onion and garlic and cook with first measure of butter on High for 3 minutes. Peel tomatoes by blanching in boiling water for 1 minute and dice. Add to cooked onion with brown sugar, oregano and salt. Cook on High for 10 minutes. Drain off any excess liquid. Cut mussels into quarters, drain prawns and stir into tomato mixture. Heat on 70% power for 4 minutes, toss halfway through cooking. Melt second measure of butter with chopped parsley on High for about 30 seconds. Arrange hot spaghetti on serving plates, top with seafood and tomato sauce. Pour over parsley and butter and sprinkle with parmesan cheese.
Serves 4.

PASTA

• SPIRALS AND CHEESE BAKE

2 slices white bread	1 teaspoon salt
¼ cup milk	4 cups cooked Diamond spirals
50 g butter	100 g gruyere cheese
150 g mushrooms	50 g grated parmesan cheese
3 eggs	100 ml cream

Remove crusts from bread, break up and pour over milk, soak 10 minutes. Melt butter on High power (100%) for about 45 seconds. Slice mushrooms, mix into butter and cook on high for 4 minutes. Beat eggs and salt. Mash bread and milk and add to mushrooms with eggs. Place half spirals in medium-sized, round dish, cover with mushrooms and egg mixture. Slice gruyere cheese and lay over mushrooms. Sprinkle with half of parmesan cheese. Cover with remaining cooked spirals. Pour over cream and sprinkle with remaining parmesan cheese. Cook covered on 70% power for 10 minutes. Brown under preheated grill. Serves 4.

• VEGETELLI IN AN EGG SAUCE

200 g Diamond vegetelli pasta	1 teaspoon curry powder
1 teaspoon oil	2 tablespoons flour
25 g butter	1 ½ cups milk
1 medium onion	1 teaspoon salt
3 cm piece root ginger	4 hard-boiled eggs
2 cloves garlic	¼ cup chopped parsley to garnish

Cook vegetelli pasta in boiling, salted water with oil for about 10 to 12 minutes, either in a saucepan or microwave on High power (100%), stirring halfway through cooking, until pasta is firm to the bite. Drain and rinse thoroughly. Cut up butter roughly. Peel and finely chop onion, ginger and garlic and cook together with curry powder on High for 3 minutes. Stir in flour and cook on High for 1 minute. Mix in milk and cook on High for about 3 minutes or until thick, stirring occasionally. Add salt. Shell eggs and cut into quarters. Gently mix cooked pasta, eggs and curry sauce together and reheat on 70% power for 3 to 4 minutes, or until piping hot. Sprinkle with chopped parsley to garnish. Serves 4.

• VEGETELLI SALAD

200 g Diamond vegetelli pasta	2 small tomatoes
1 teaspoon oil	3 tablespoons mayonnaise
2 rashers lean bacon	2 tablespoons orange juice
2 hard-boiled eggs	¼ teaspoon salt

Cook vegetelli pasta in boiling, salted water with oil for about 10 to 12 minutes, either in a saucepan or microwave on High power (100%) stirring halfway through cooking, until pasta is firm to the bite. Drain and rinse thoroughly. Remove rind from bacon. Cover with a paper towel and cook on High for 2 to 3 minutes until crisp. Cut into thin strips. Shell eggs and cut into wedges. Cut tomatoes into wedges. Mix together mayonnaise, orange juice and salt, pour over pasta and combine. Add bacon, eggs and tomatoes and toss lightly. Chill before serving. Serves 4.

Small amounts of food cook better than large amounts in the microwave.

• VEGETABLE LASAGNE

300 g Diamond lasagne
1 teaspoon oil
25 g butter
3 tablespoons flour
1 ½ cups milk
1 cup grated tasty cheese
2 eggs

1 teaspoon salt
500 g frozen mixed vegetables
300 mls tomato juice
2 teaspoons sugar
2 tablespoons grated parmesan
    cheese

Cook lasagne in boiling, salted water with oil for about 10 to 12 minutes, either in a saucepan or microwave on High power (100%) stirring halfway through, cooking until pasta is firm to the bite. Drain and rinse thoroughly. Melt butter on High for about 30 seconds. Stir in flour and cook a further 30 seconds on High. Mix in milk and cook on High for about 3 minutes, or until thick, stirring occasionally. Blend in cheese. Beat eggs and add to sauce with a little of the measured salt to taste. Rinse frozen vegetables in cold water, drain well and mix in with tomato juice, sugar and remaining salt. Use one-third of vegetable mixture to cover bottom of large rectangular microwave dish, lay over one-third cooked lasagne and pour over one-third cheese sauce. Continue with layers of remaining ingredients in same order. Cover with lid or microwave-safe plastic wrap and cook on 70% power for 30 minutes. Sprinkle with grated parmesan and brown under hot grill.
Serves 4.

Cooking times will depend on the material of the cooking vessel. If you deviate from that specified in a recipe, the cooking time will probably differ.

• BAKED ORANGE ROUGHY

25 g butter
2 cloves garlic
500 g orange roughy fillets
2 tablespoons chopped parsley

1 tablespoon lemon juice
¼ teaspoon salt
Pepper

Melt butter on High power (100%) for about 30 seconds. Crush and peel garlic, mix into melted butter and use to liberally brush both sides of fish. Arrange fish on a flat microwave dish with thicker parts to outside and thin ends of fillets tucked underneath other pieces of fish. Sprinkle chopped parsley, lemon juice, salt and pepper over fish and cook on 70% power for about 6 minutes, rearranging fish halfway through cooking.
Serves 4.

• CRUNCHY TOPPED FISH

500 g skinned and boned terakihi
25 g butter
½ small onion
2 tablespoons crunchy peanut butter

½ teaspoon salt
Pepper
1 tablespoon finely chopped parsley

Arrange fish in a flat microwave dish, thicker parts to the outside. Melt butter on High power (100%) for about 30 seconds. Peel and finely chop onion, add to butter and cook on High for 2 minutes. Stir in peanut butter, salt, pepper and parsley. Spread this mixture evenly over fish. Cover dish loosely with grease-proof paper and cook on High for 4 to 5 minutes, rearranging fillets halfway through cooking.
Serves 4.

• CURRIED SQUID RINGS

4 squid tubes
2 tablespoons olive oil

2 cloves garlic
1 teaspoon curry powder

Cut squid tubes into thin rings. Add olive oil and toss to coat. Peel and finely chop garlic. Add to squid rings with curry powder and mix well. Leave to marinate about 1 hour. Preheat a browning dish for maximum suggested time. Add squid rings and toss constantly until sizzling stops. Cook on 50% power for about 2 minutes, tossing halfway through. Squid should be soft and just cooked.
Serves 4.

• FISH KEBABS

400 g orange roughy fillets
1 tablespoon olive oil
1 teaspoon lemon juice
¹/₈ teaspoon salt

100 g small broccoli florets
225 g can pineapple chunks
1 teaspoon oil
1 teaspoon water

Trim fish and cut into cubes about 3cm square. Mix together first measure of olive oil, lemon juice and salt and marinate fish cubes for about 1 hour. Using wooden skewers assemble eight kebabs with cubes of fish, broccoli and drained pineapple. Mix together second measure of oil and water and use to lightly brush broccoli florets. Place over a flat microwave dish and cook on 70% power for 10 minutes, rearranging kebabs halfway through the cooking time.
Serves 4.

• FISH PATÉ

½ onion
350 g skinned and boned gurnard
250 g pot sour cream
1 egg

½ cup grated cheese
Salt
Pepper

Peel and roughly chop onion. Place in a small microwave dish and cook on High power (100%) for 2 minutes. Place onion, fish, sour cream, egg, grated cheese, salt and pepper in a food processor and mix until smooth. Place in a small microwave ring mould, smooth top. Cover with microwave-safe plastic wrap and cook on 50% power for about 15 minutes. Paté should be just firm. Leave to cool in mould before turning out.
Serves 4.

• FRESH SALMON SALAD

200 g fresh salmon steaks
1 tablespoon lemon juice
3 small courgettes
1 tablespoon water
2 tomatoes
2 tablespoons oil

1 tablespoon vinegar
½ teaspoon salt
Pepper
2 hard-boiled eggs
Lettuce

Place salmon steaks in a small microwave casserole and sprinkle with lemon juice. Cover with microwave-safe plastic wrap and cook on 70% power for 1 minute. Turn over, cover and cook on 70% power for a further 1 minute. Leave to stand with film in place for 5 minutes. Drain salmon, remove skin and bones and break into chunks. Trim courgettes and cut into rings. Sprinkle over water. Cover and cook on High for 2 minutes or until slightly crunchy. Drain. Cut tomatoes into segments. Mix together oil, vinegar, salt and pepper. Add tomatoes, courgettes and salmon chunks and toss to coat. Peel and slice hard-boiled eggs, add to salad and carefully mix together. Chill well. Serve over lettuce.
Serves 3-4.

• FRIED FISH SAVOURIES

300 g white fish fillets
1 rasher bacon
2 spring onions
½ beaten egg
2 teaspoons DYC soy sauce

2 teaspoons cornflour
1 French stick
Soft butter
1 tomato

Mince or very finely chop fish. Finely chop bacon and cook on High power (100%) for 1 minute. Trim and finely chop spring onions. Mix together minced fish, cooked bacon, spring onions, egg, soy sauce and cornflour. Cut bread into slices about 1.5cm thick and spread evenly with butter on both sides. Arrange in a circle on a microwave plate and precook eight slices of bread at a time on High for 2 minutes. Put dessertspoonfuls of fish mixture on bread slices, spread out and cook eight at a time on High for 2 minutes or until crisp. Chop tomato and use to garnish fish savouries.

For foods that have thick and thin ends such as some fish, broccoli and chicken pieces, place the thickest part to the outside of the dish.

FISH

• HAPUKA STEAKS ON A BED OF VEGETABLES

1 small onion	2 small courgettes
1 carrot	2 tomatoes
2 cloves garlic	¼ teaspoon salt
100 g small mushrooms	Pepper
1 tablespoon water	4 hapuka steaks
1 tablespoon oil	1 tablespoon oil

Peel onion and cut into thin rings. Peel carrot and cut into sticks. Crush and peel garlic. Wipe and halve mushrooms. Toss together onion, carrot, garlic, mushrooms, water and first measure of oil in a large microwave dish. Cover and cook on High power (100%) for 1 minute. Cut courgettes into thin sticks. Add to onion and carrot mixture. Cover and cook on High for 2 minutes. Peel tomatoes and cut into wedges. Add to vegetable mixture, season and toss well. Cover and cook on High for 3 minutes. At this stage vegetables are still crunchy; cook longer if preferred. Keep warm. Brush fish steaks with second measure of olive oil. Cover with greaseproof paper and cook on 70% power for 10 minutes. Serve immediately on the vegetables.
Serves 4.

• KUMARA AND SMOKED FISH LAYER PIE

500 g kumaras	150 g broccoli
¼ cup water	450 g can creamed corn
310 g can smoked fish fillets	½ teaspoon paprika

Peel kumaras, slice thickly and sprinkle with water. Cover and cook on High power (100%) for 7 to 8 minutes or until just soft, stirring halfway through cooking. Arrange kumaras on a microwave pie dish. Drain and flake fish fillets and place in a layer over kumara. Cut broccoli into small florets, cover and cook on High for about 3 minutes or until tender. Arrange over fish. Spoon over corn evenly and sprinkle with paprika. Cook uncovered on 70% power for about 7 minutes or until heated through.
Serves 4.

• MUSSELS IN A GARLIC WINE SAUCE

4 spring onions	¼ teaspoon salt
3 cloves garlic	Pepper
25 g butter	20 - 24 live mussels in shells
½ cup dry white wine	¼ cup cream

Finely slice spring onions. Crush, peel and finely chop the garlic. Melt butter on High power (100%) for about 30 seconds. Add spring onion and garlic and cook on High for 1 minute. Gradually blend in wine, salt and pepper and heat on High for 1 minute. Wash, scrub and remove beards from mussels. Place half of mussels in large casserole dish, add wine sauce, toss and cook on High for 4 to 5 minutes until just opened, rearranging halfway through cooking. Remove with slotted spoon and keep hot. Add remaining mussels, toss in sauce and cook on High for about 4 minutes. Remove mussels and release from the shells then replace in half shells. Stir cream into wine liquor. Arrange in a microwave serving dish and cook on 30% power for about 20 seconds to heat through. Pour sauce over mussels and serve at once.
Serves 4.

The denser the texture of a food the longer the cooking process carries on after food is taken from the oven.

• SEAFOOD STUFFED PANCAKES

½ onion
25 g butter
2 tablespoons flour
1 cup milk
100 g smoked fish

100 g smoked oysters in oil
2 tablespoons finely chopped chives
½ teaspoon paprika
8 cooked pancakes

Peel and chop onion. In a medium-sized jug cook together onion and butter on High power (100%) for 1 ½ minutes. Stir in flour and cook on High a further 30 seconds. Blend in milk and cook on High for 3 minutes, stirring every minute. Chop smoked fish. Drain and halve oysters. Mix fish, oysters, chives and paprika into sauce and use to fill pancakes. Place filled pancakes in a flat microwave dish. Cover and cook on 50% power for about 8 minutes or until heated through.
Serves 4.

• SMOKED FISH PIE

1 small onion
25 g butter
2 tablespoons flour
1 cup milk
2 hard-boiled eggs
185 g can smoked fish fillets

2 tablespoons finely chopped parsley
700 g potatoes
¼ cup water
½ cup milk
25 g butter
½ teaspoon salt

Peel and chop the onion. Melt butter on High power (100%) for about 30 seconds. Add onion and cook on High for 2 minutes. Stir in flour and cook on High for 1 minute. Blend in milk and cook on High for 3 minutes or until thick, stirring every minute. Peel and roughly chop hard-boiled eggs. Drain smoked fish fillets. Add to sauce with eggs and parsley, mix to combine. Peel potatoes and cut into large chunks. Add water. Cover and cook on High for about 12 minutes or until tender, stirring once. Drain potatoes, mash and beat in milk, butter and salt. Pour fish sauce into a medium-sized microwave baking dish and cover with layer of mashed potato. Smooth top. Cover with microwave-safe plastic wrap and cook on 70% power for 10 minutes.
Serves 3 to 4.

• STUFFED WHOLE FISH

1 medium-sized whole fish, e.g. mullet
Salt
½ small onion
1 teaspoon olive oil
¼ cup toasted breadcrumbs
2 tablespoons coconut

1 tablespoon finely chopped parsley
1 tablespoon sesame seeds
1 tablespoon tomato sauce
¼ teaspoon salt
Pepper
2 tablespoons butter

Rub cavity of fish with salt to clean. Peel and finely chop onion. Place in a microwave bowl or jug with olive oil and cook on High power (100%) for 1 minute. Stir in breadcrumbs, coconut, parsley, sesame seeds, tomato sauce, salt and pepper and use to stuff fish. Prick skin of fish and dot surface with butter then loosely wrap in lightly oiled greaseproof paper or baking paper and fold in ends. Place on a flat microwave dish or plate and cook for about 10 minutes on 70% power, turning over halfway through cooking. Time will vary depending on size of fish. Use a fork to check if flesh will flake easily. Flounder can also be used for this recipe. Cook on High for 3 ½ minutes for each stuffed flounder.
Serves 4.

FISH

• TUNA BAKE

2 potatoes
1 onion
1 small green pepper
100 g mushrooms
185 g can tuna
2 tablespoons butter

2 tablespoons flour
1 cup milk
Salt
Freshly ground black pepper
1 cup grated cheese

Wash the potatoes and prick the skins with a fork. Cook on High power (100%) for 5 minutes. Peel and slice potatoes and arrange on the bottom of a deep casserole dish. Peel and finely dice the onion. Arrange on top of the potato. Deseed and finely chop the green pepper. Place on top of the onion. Wipe and slice the mushrooms and place on top of the green pepper. Drain the tuna and break up the large pieces. Place over the mushrooms. In a large glass microwave jug, melt the butter on High for 30 seconds. Stir in the flour and milk. Cook on High for 3 to 4 minutes until thick. Season with salt and pepper and stir in the grated cheese. Pour sauce over the vegetables and fish. Cover with microwave-safe plastic wrap and cook on High for 7 minutes. Place under grill until golden if wished.
Serves 4.

• TUNA AND SPINACH LOAF

10 to 12 leaves spinach
2 cloves garlic
1 onion
1 tablespoon butter
440 g can tuna in brine
½ green pepper

1 tomato
3 tablespoons chopped parsley
2 tablespoons sweet chilli sauce
4 eggs
1 cup cooked brown rice
Freshly ground black pepper

Trim the tough stalks from the spinach leaves. Wash well. Place spinach on a plate and cover with microwave-safe plastic wrap. Microwave on High power (100%) for 2½ minutes. Crush, peel and mash the garlic to a paste. Peel and finely chop the onion. Put the butter, onion and garlic into a bowl and cover. Cook on High for 1½ minutes. Put the tuna and brine in a bowl and flake with a fork. Finely chop the pepper and tomato. Add the onion, pepper, tomato, parsley, chilli sauce, eggs and rice to the fish. Season with pepper and mix well. Reserve two to three spinach leaves and use the remainder to line the base and sides of a six-cup capacity microwave glass loaf dish. Spoon the filling into the loaf dish. Cover with remaining spinach leaves. Cover with microwave-safe plastic wrap. Elevate and cook on 70% power for 18 to 20 minutes or until the loaf has almost set in the middle. Stand 10 minutes. Turn out and serve hot or cold. Serves 6.

• VEGETABLE TOPPED FISH

4 skinned and boned white fish fillets
2 tablespoons lemon juice
1 carrot
1 courgette

2 spring onions
1 tablespoon soy sauce
Watercress to garnish

Place fish in a shallow microwave dish. Sprinkle with lemon juice. Peel carrot and cut into thin sticks. Wash courgette and cut into thin strips. Trim the spring onions and slice finely. Mix the carrots, courgettes and spring onions with the soy sauce and place on fish fillets. Cook on High power (100%) for 10 minutes or until fish is tender. Serves 4.

Choose even-sized foods for easier more even cooking.

• ALMOND CHICKEN

1 onion
1 tablespoon oil
½ cup fresh brown breadcrumbs
½ cup sliced almonds
1 teaspoon grated lemon rind
About 2 tablespoons milk

Salt
Freshly ground black pepper
No. 5 chicken
1 tablespoon DYC soy sauce
2 tablespoons red wine

Peel and finely chop the onion. Place the onion and oil in a glass microwave jug. Microwave on High power (100%) for 4 minutes. Add the breadcrumbs, sliced almonds and lemon rind. Add enough milk to bind the mixture together. Season with salt and pepper. Spoon the stuffing into the cavity of the chicken. Sew together the openings or secure with wooden toothpicks. Truss the chicken with cotton string. Place chicken in a microwave baking dish with a lid. Brush with soy sauce and add the red wine to the dish. Cover. Microwave on High for 18 to 20 minutes or until the chicken is cooked. Spoon juices over the chicken twice during cooking time.
Serves 3 to 4.

• CHICKEN CURRY

1 medium onion
25 g butter
2 teaspoons curry powder
1 tablespoon flour
4 chicken pieces

1 cooking apple
¼ teaspoon dried marjoram
½ cup chutney
¼ cup natural unsweetened yoghurt

Peel and chop the onion. Melt butter on High power (100%) for about 30 seconds. Add onion and cook on High for 2 minutes. Stir in curry powder and flour and cook on High for 1 minute. Remove skin from chicken pieces. Peel, core and dice the apple. Add chicken, apple, marjoram and chutney to onion mixture. Cover and cook on High for 6 minutes. Turn chicken pieces around and over. Cover dish and cook on High for about 6 minutes. Chicken should be just cooked at this stage. Stir in yoghurt and cook at 50% power for 4 minutes or until heated through.
Serves 4.

• CHICKEN FRICASSEE

1 cooked No. 7 chicken
1 onion
2 tablespoons clarified butter
2 tablespoons flour

1 cup chicken stock
310 g can red kidney beans
1 teaspoon chopped fresh herbs
Chopped parsley to garnish

Remove flesh from chicken and cut into bite-sized pieces. Peel and thinly slice the onion. Place onions in a microwave dish with clarified butter. Cover and cook on High power (100%) for 2 minutes. Stir in the flour then the stock. Microwave on High for 4 minutes. Drain and add the beans and herbs to the chicken. Stir and cook on High for 2 minutes. Garnish with parsley.
Serves 6.

POULTRY

• CHICKEN IN CRANBERRY SAUCE

1 medium onion
25 g butter
4 chicken pieces
1 tablespoon DYC soy sauce

1 tablespoon lemon juice
¼ teaspoon dried oregano
¾ cup cranberry sauce

Peel and finely chop onion. Melt butter on High power (100%) for about 30 seconds. Add onion and cook on High for 3 minutes. Remove skin from chicken pieces. Add chicken, soy sauce, lemon juice, oregano and cranberry sauce to onion mixture. Cover and cook on High for 7 minutes. Turn chicken pieces around and over. Cover dish and cook on High for about 7 minutes or until juices run clear. Stand a few minutes, stir and serve.
Serves 4.

• CHICKEN PATÉ

1 large onion
2 cloves garlic
2 rashers bacon
1 tablespoon butter
200 g chicken livers

250 g cooked chicken
2 eggs
¼ teaspoon salt
White pepper

Peel and roughly chop onion and garlic. Remove the rind and dice bacon. Melt the butter on High power (100%) for about 30 seconds. Add onion, garlic and bacon and cook on High for 4 minutes. Remove any sinews from chicken livers, place in a small bowl. Cover with a paper towel and cook on High for 4 minutes. Break cooked chicken into small pieces. Place onion mixture, chicken livers, cooked chicken, eggs, salt and pepper in a food processor, blender or mincer and mix to a smooth paste. Pour into a lightly buttered one-litre microwave dish. Cover and cook on 50% power for 10 minutes or until set. Leave covered until completely cold.
Serves 8 to 10.

• CHICKEN STROGANOFF

No. 6 cooked chicken
1 onion
3 cups roughly chopped mushrooms
3 tablespoons sherry

½ cup sour cream
Freshly ground black pepper
Salt

Remove the chicken flesh from the bones. Peel and finely chop the onion. Cook the onion on High power (100%) for 2 minutes. Add the chicken and mushrooms and cook on High for a further 5 minutes. Stir in the sherry and sour cream, freshly ground black pepper and salt. Stand covered for 5 minutes.
Serves 4 to 6.

Always elevate a roast — cook in an oven bag or covered dish. When roasting vegetables cut pumpkin larger than potato and set the kumara in the centre of the dish.

• CHINESE SOY CHICKEN

3 cm piece root ginger
2 tablespoons honey
2 tablespoons sherry
2 tablespoons DYC soy sauce
1 teaspoon five spice powder

½ teaspoon salt
1 No. 7 chicken
2 cloves garlic
½ cup DYC soy sauce
½ cup water

Peel ginger and grate finely. Warm honey on High power (100%) for about 20 seconds or until melted. Mix together ginger, honey, sherry, first measure of soy sauce, five spice powder and salt. Pour over chicken and inside cavity. Leave to marinate I hour or more turning occasionally. Peel and chop garlic. Mix together second measure of soy sauce, water and garlic in a large deep microwave casserole and heat on High for 3 minutes. Add marinated chicken and marinade. Cover and cook on 70% power for 13 to 15 minutes. Turn and cook at 70% power for a further 13 to 15 minutes. Leave covered in juices and turn occasionally for about 10 minutes before cutting and serving.
Serves 4.

• CREAMY PEPPER CHICKEN

1 onion
25 g butter
4 single boneless chicken breasts
1 tablespoon cornflour
2 tablespoons water

1 tablespoon tomato paste
½ x 250 g pot sour cream
1 tablespoon pickled green peppercorns
¼ teaspoon salt

Peel and finely chop onion. Melt butter in a shallow microwave casserole dish on High power (100%) for 1 to 1½ minutes. Add onion. Cook on High for 2½ minutes. Remove skins from chicken breasts. Trim off any excess fat. Cut each breast into 1.5 cm slices, cutting across the grain. Arrange each sliced breast on the cooked onions. Cover and cook on High for 3 minutes. Leave to stand. In a small bowl mix cornflour and water to a paste. Add tomato paste, sour cream, peppercorns and salt. Pour sauce over chicken and onions. Cover with microwave safe wrap. Puncture two holes in the wrap. Cook on High for 3 to 4 minutes, or until chicken is cooked. Stand 5 minutes. Stir and serve with rice.
Serves 4.

• CURRY AND APPLE CHICKEN

1 onion
1 tablespoon curry powder
¾ cup coconut cream

8 chicken drumsticks
1 green apple

Peel and finely dice the onion. Mix the onion, curry powder and coconut cream together. Place the chicken drumsticks in a microwave dish. Pour over the coconut mixture. Cover and cook on High power (100%) for 10 minutes. Core the apple and cut into wedges. Add to the chicken and cook on High for 2 minutes. Stand covered for 5 minutes.
Serves 4.

If cooking uneven meats cover the thinner parts with foil part way through cooking to prevent further cooking.

POULTRY

• GINGER DRUMSTICKS

3 spring onions
1 tablespoon oil
1 teaspoon finely chopped root ginger
8 chicken drumsticks
1 cup chicken stock

2 tablespoons sugar
2 tablespoons DYC vinegar
1 tablespoon DYC soy sauce
1 tablespoon oyster sauce
1 tablespoon cornflour

Slice spring onions finely on the diagonal. Place oil in a microwave dish. Heat on High power (100%) for 10 seconds. Add spring onions and toss well to coat in oil. Add ginger. Arrange chicken in dish. Turn to coat in oil. Cook on 70% power for 10 minutes turning once. Add chicken stock, cover and cook a further 10 minutes on 70% power. Combine sugar, vinegar, soy sauce, oyster sauce and cornflour. Stir into chicken mixture. Return to microwave and cook covered on High for 4 minutes or until chicken is cooked.
Serves 4.

• HOT CHICKEN SALAD

1 No. 5 chicken
Melted butter

1 tablespoon chopped fresh marjoram
1 tablespoon chopped parsley

VINAIGRETTE:

½ cup olive oil
¼ cup DYC spiced vinegar
1 teaspoon sugar

¼ teaspoon curry powder
Salt
Freshly ground black pepper.

Wash chicken and dry with paper towel. Brush with melted butter. Place chicken on a rack in a microwave dish. Cook on 70% power for 26-30 minutes, turning halfway through cooking. Leave to stand 10 minutes. Remove skin and break chicken into large pieces. Toss in vinaigrette. Sprinkle with chopped marjoram and parsley. Serve hot.
Serves 4.

VINAIGRETTE:

Place oil, vinegar, sugar, curry powder, salt and pepper in a screw top jar. Shake well.

• LEMON AND SPRING ONION CHICKEN

1 clove garlic
4 chicken pieces
¼ cup lemon juice
¼ cup tomato sauce

½ teaspoon grated root ginger
1 tablespoon honey
2 spring onions

Crush, peel and finely chop the garlic. Place the chicken in a microwave dish. Add the lemon juice, tomato sauce, garlic, ginger and honey. Baste the chicken so as all the pieces are coated. Cook on High power (100%) for 14 minutes, or until juices run clear. Stir once or twice during cooking. Finely slice the spring onions and add to the chicken. Stand covered for 5 minutes and stir before serving.
Serves 4

Always choose a time option that undercooks the food cooked in the microwave. It is simple to add time to complete cooking.

• MEXICAN CHICKEN

1 onion
2 cloves garlic
1 tablespoon oil
¼ teaspoon ground mixed spice
¼ teaspoon chilli powder

½ cup peanuts
4 chicken pieces
425 g can tomatoes in juice
2 tablespoons tomato concentrate
¾ cup tinned whole kernel corn

Peel onion and garlic and chop finely. Mix in oil, spice and chilli powder and cook on High power (100%) for 3 minutes. Roast peanuts on High for 4 to 5 minutes, shaking the dish occasionally. Chop the peanuts roughly. Remove skin from chicken, chop the tomatoes. Add chicken, nuts, tomatoes and juice, tomato concentrate and corn to onion mixture. Cook on High for 15 to 20 minutes or until cooked, rearranging chicken halfway through cooking.
Serves 4.

• OATY DRUMSTICKS

8 chicken drumsticks
1 egg
2 teaspoons olive oil
2 tablespoons Flemings oat bran
¼ cup toasted breadcrumbs

1 tablespoon paprika
1 tablespoon grated parmesan cheese
¼ teaspoon salt
White pepper

Make a circular cut in chicken skin at thinnest part of drumstick, then peel off skin from thickest end to cut. Beat egg with olive oil. Mix together oatbran, toasted crumbs, paprika, parmesan cheese, salt and pepper. Dip drumsticks in beaten egg and oil, then into crumb mixture. Arrange chicken in cartwheel fashion on roasting rack or large plate, making sure thicker parts are to the outside. Cook on High power (100%) for about 8 minutes for small drumsticks, about 12 minutes for larger drumsticks, or until chicken flesh has lost its pink colour and juices run clear.
Serves 4.

• SESAME CHICKEN

2 tablespoons soy sauce
2 tablespoons brown sugar
1 tablespoon DYC vinegar

1 No. 6 chicken
2 tablespoons sesame seeds

Combine soy sauce, brown sugar and vinegar. Place chicken on a microwave plate. Pour over soy mixture. Sprinkle sesame seeds over. Microwave on 70% power for 26-30 minutes or until juices run clear when tested with a skewer. Baste twice during cooking with soy mixture and turn chicken halfway through cooking. Leave to stand for 5 minutes.
Serves 3 to 4.

• TASTY CHICKEN PIECES

4 chicken pieces
2 tablespoon flour
1 teaspoon mixed herbs

1 teaspoon chicken flavoured stock
1 teaspoon bacon flavoured stock

Mix flour, herbs and flavoured stock. Wet chicken, puncture skin in several places, coat with seasoned mixture and arrange on a plate with the thickest parts nearest the rim. Stand 10 minutes. Microwave on High power (100%) for 6-8 minutes.
Serves 3-4.

A covered roast will keep hot for about 30 minutes after cooking.

• BEEF AND LAMB CASSEROLE

500 g topside	Salt
250 g lamb leg steaks	Freshly ground black pepper
300 g bacon pieces	1 bay leaf
½ cup red wine	2 tablespoons flour
1½ cups beef stock	¼ cup water
¾ teaspoon ground nutmeg	

Cut topside, lamb and bacon pieces into 2cm cubes. Place in a microwave dish. Pour over red wine, beef stock, nutmeg, salt, freshly ground black pepper and bay leaf. Cover and cook on 50% power for 40 minutes. Mix flour and water together to a smooth paste. Add to meat dish, mix well. Cook for a further 10 minutes on 70% power.
Serves 4.

• BEEF CASSEROLE

2 onions	150 g button mushrooms
3 cloves garlic	1 bay leaf
750 g blade steak	3 tablespoons Fielders cornflour
¼ cup red wine	¼ cup water
430 g can beef consomme	

Peel and roughly chop the onions. Crush, peel and mash the garlic to a paste. Trim fat from the meat. In a large microwave casserole, combine the onions, garlic, meat and wine. Leave for 1 hour. Add the consomme, stirring to mix. Wipe and trim the mushrooms. Add to the casserole with the bay leaf. Cover and microwave on High power (100%) for 10 minutes. Reduce the heat to 50% power and cook a further 30 minutes. Remove from the microwave and remove the bay leaf. Mix the cornflour and water together. Add to the casserole and stir well to mix. Return to the microwave and cook on High for 5 minutes. Stand 10 minutes.
Serves 4-6.

• BEEF KEBABS

400 g rump steak	
2 cloves garlic	16 pitted prunes
1 tablespoon olive oil	2 tablespoons stock or wine
¼ teaspoon dried oregano	16 button mushrooms
¼ teaspoon microwave meat seasoning	16 bay leaves

Trim meat and cut into 3cm cubes. Peel and crush garlic. Mix together meat, garlic, oil, oregano and seasoning and leave to marinate 1 to 2 hours. Soak prunes in stock or wine for about 1 hour. Assemble eight kebabs using wooden or bamboo skewers by threading meat, prunes, mushrooms and bay leaves onto each skewer. Place over a large flat dish and cook at 70% power for 6 minutes. Rearrange kebabs so that outer ones are in the centre and vice versa. Cook at 70% power for another 6 minutes or until steak is cooked to your liking.
Serves 4.

• BEEF STROGONOFF

500 g schnitzel
¼ cup seasoned flour
2 onions
2 cloves garlic
100 g mushrooms
2 tablespoons oil

2½ teaspoons prepared mustard
½ cup beef stock
½ cup white wine
¼ cup sour cream
Freshly ground black pepper
Salt

Cut the meat into thin strips and toss in the seasoned flour. Peel and finely slice the onions. Crush, peel and mash the garlic. Finely slice the mushrooms. Heat a deep browning dish on High power (100%) for maximum time recommended. Add the oil and meat. Cook on High for 3 minutes turning frequently. Add the onions, garlic, mushrooms, mustard, beef stock and wine. Return to microwave and cook on 70% power for 6 minutes turning frequently. Stir in the sour cream. Season with pepper and salt.   Serves 4.

• BEEF WITH BLACK BEAN SAUCE

500 g topside steak
1 tablespoon DYC soy sauce
1 tablespooon oyster sauce
2 tablespoons oil
2 tablespoons Chinese black beans
½ cup water

½ onion
150 g green beans
1 tablespoon Fielders cornflour
1 tablespoon sherry
¼ to ½ cup water

Trim meat and cut into thin strips. Mix in soy sauce, oyster sauce and one tablespoon of oil and marinate about 1 hour. Soak black beans in first measure of water. Preheat browning dish for maximum recommended time. Seal marinated meat on all sides and cook on High power (100%) for about 3 minutes or until just cooked. Keep meat hot and reserve meat juices. Peel the onion, quarter and separate the layers. Toss with remaining oil and cook on High for 1 minute. Top and tail beans, cut into 3cm lengths. Stir into onions and cook on High for 2 minutes or until done to your liking. Keep hot. Drain black beans, rinse well and mash with a fork. Mix together cornflour, sherry and water. Add black beans and reserved meat juices. Stir well and cook on High for 3 minutes or until thick, stirring once. Toss together meat, vegetables and sauce before serving. Reheat if necessary on 70% power.   Serves 4.

• BOBOTIE

1 large onion
500 g minced steak
2 teaspoons curry powder
1 teaspoon turmeric
1 teaspoon salt
1 cooking apple
2 slices brown bread

2 tablespoons lemon juice
3 tablespoons seedless raisins
3 tablespoons coconut
3 bay leaves
1 egg
1 cup milk

Peel and slice the onion. Break up and add mince with curry powder, turmeric and salt and cook on High power (100%) or 3 minutes. Peel, core and dice the apple, stir into mince and cook on High for 2 minutes or until mince has lost its pink colour. Make bread into crumbs and add to mince mixture with the lemon juice, seedless raisins and coconut. Mix well and turn into a round dish, level top and add bay leaves. Beat egg with the milk and pour over meat. Elevate and cook on 50% power for about 25 minutes or until milk and egg mixture is set. Serves 4-6.

MEAT

• CHILLI PEPPER BEEF

1 tablespoon brown sugar
2 tablespoons *Fielders* cornflour
1 tablespoon DYC white vinegar
½ teaspoon salt
½ cup water
750 g topside mince

1 large onion
5 dried chillies
½ green pepper
2 tablespoons chilli sauce
2 tablespoons tomato paste
310 g can red kidney beans

Mix together the sugar, cornflour, vinegar, salt and water. Set aside. Place the mince in a large microwave dish and break up. Peel and slice the onion and chop the chillies. Add onion and chillies to beef. Cover and cook on High power (100%) for 6 to 7 minutes or until meat loses its pinkness, stirring every 2 minutes with a fork to break up mince. Drain any excess fat from dish. Deseed and slice the pepper. Add the pepper, chilli sauce and tomato paste to the dish. Stir to mix. Add the cornflour mixture. Cook uncovered on High for 4 to 5 minutes or until mixture has thickened. Drain kidney beans, add to meat. Cook on High for a further 1½ minutes. Stand 5 minutes.
Serves 4.

• CHINESE PORK BUNS

2 rashers bacon
1 onion
1 clove garlic
¼ teaspoon salt
1 teaspoon clarified butter
250 g pork mince
1 tablespoon flour

1½ teaspoons paprika
100 ml chicken stock
1 tablespoon sour cream
1 tablespoon lemon juice
Salt
Freshly ground black pepper

Remove rind from the bacon and roughly chop the flesh. Peel and finely chop the onion. Crush, peel and mash the garlic with the salt. Put the bacon, onion, garlic and butter into a microwave dish. Microwave on High power (100%) for 2 minutes. Add the pork mince, microwave on High for 2 minutes. Stir in the flour and paprika. Microwave for a further 1 minute. Gradually add the chicken stock. Return to the microwave and cook on High for a further 3 minutes. Leave pork mixture until cold. Stir in the sour cream and lemon juice. Season with salt and pepper. Divide the dough into ten equal portions and roll each portion into a ball. On a lightly floured surface, roll each ball into a 12cm circle. Brush the edge with water. Put a tablespoon of pork filling into the centre of each circle. Draw the edges of the dough into the centre pressing together firmly to form a bun. Put the buns into a microwave dish, drawn edge uppermost. Add 1 teaspoon of water to dish. Cover and microwave on High for 3 minutes. Turn the buns over and cook for a further 2 minutes. Stand 1 minute.
Makes 10.

DOUGH:

1½ cups flour
½ teaspoon Edmonds baking powder
1½ tablespoons oil

100 ml warm water
1 teaspoon DYC white vinegar

Sift flour and baking powder into a bowl. Add the oil, water and vinegar, stir to a soft, pliable dough. Wrap the dough and leave to rest 20 minutes. Knead lightly before using.

Always use microwave-safe plastic wrap for microwave cooking. This is marked on the box or wrapper.

• CITRUS LAMB

¼ cup marmalade	1 fillet from loin of lamb
2 tablespoons DYC soy sauce	2 tablespoons white wine
2 tablespoons brown sugar	

Mix the marmalade, soy sauce and brown sugar together. Marinate the meat in the marmalade mixture for 2 hours. Remove the lamb from the marinade reserving the marinade. Place meat on a microwave plate and cover with a paper towel. Cook on High power (100%) for 5½ minutes. Stand 2 minutes. Add the wine to the marinade. Cook on High for about 45 seconds or until hot. Serve lamb finely sliced with the hot marinade.
Serves 4.

• CORNED BEEF WITH MUSTARD SAUCE

1 kg corned beef	1 bayleaf
2 tablespoons brown sugar	1½ teaspoons peppercorns
2 tablespoons DYC vinegar	4 cups hot water
1 teaspoon whole cloves	1 onion

Rinse corned beef. Place corned beef in a large microwave casserole dish. Add brown sugar, vinegar, cloves, bay leaf peppercorns and hot water. Peel and quarter onion. Add to casserole. Cover and microwave on High power (100%) for 10 minutes. Turn meat over and cook on 50% power for 1 hour. Leave to stand in cooking liquid for 15 minutes before serving. Reserve one cup of the cooking liquor for the sauce. Serve with mustard sauce.
Serves 4 to 6.

MUSTARD SAUCE:

1 tablespoon *Fielders* cornflour	White pepper
4 tablespoons brown sugar	1 egg
1¾ teaspoons dry mustard	¼ cup DYC vinegar
Salt	1 cup corned beef cooking liquor

Place cornflour, brown sugar, mustard, salt and pepper in a microwave bowl. Lightly beat egg. Add vinegar and corned beef cooking liquor, beating to combine. Slowly add liquid to dry ingredients, mixing well to form a smooth mixture. Cover and microwave on High power (100%) for 4 minutes, stirring once during cooking.

• CURRIED MEATBALLS WITH MINT

1 onion	Salt
1 clove garlic	Freshly ground black pepper
500 g topside mince	1 tablespoon tomato sauce
1 egg	Extra chopped mint
2½ teaspoons mild curry powder	Natural unsweetened yoghurt
1 tablespoon chopped fresh mint	

Peel and finely chop the onion. Crush and peel garlic. Combine onion, garlic, mince, egg, curry powder, mint, salt, pepper and tomato sauce. Mix well. Roll into 5cm balls. Arrange evenly spaced on a paper towel around the outside edge of a dinner plate. Microwave on 70% power for 8 minutes, turning halfway through cooking. Serve scattered with chopped mint and yoghurt.
Serves 4.

Only use plastics designed for microwave use. Many plastics contain impurities and cannot be used safely in the microwave.

• CURRIED LAMB MINCE AND PINEAPPLE

1 onion	½ teaspoon dried sage
3 medium carrots	225g can unsweetened pineapple
1 green pepper	chunks
200 g mushrooms	1 tablespoon *Fielders* cornflour
2 tablespoons water	½ teaspoon salt
500 g lamb mince	Pepper
2 teaspoons curry powder	1 cup grated cheese

Peel the onion and cut into rings. Peel and dice the carrots. Remove seeds from the green pepper and slice flesh. Slice mushrooms. Mix together onion, carrots, green pepper and mushrooms with water, cover and cook on High power (100%) for 6 to 8 minutes, or until vegetables are just soft, stirring halfway through cooking. Drain cooking liquid and reserve. Break up mince, mix in curry powder and sage and cook on High for 5 minutes, stirring occasionally. Drain juice from pineapple and use quarter of a cup to mix with cornflour and vegetable cooking liquid. Cook on High for 2 minutes or until thickened, stirring halfway through cooking. Add salt and pepper and stir into cooked meat with pineapple chunks. Place half of vegetable mixture in a flat microwave dish, spread over half of the meat mixture. Repeat with a layer of vegetables and meat and sprinkle with cheese. Cook on High for 5 to 6 minutes.
Serves 4-6.

• CURRIED PORK

1 onion	½ cup mango chutney
50 g butter	½ cup cream
2 teaspoons curry powder	1 tablespoon *Fielders* cornflour
1 pork fillet, about 350 g	1 tablespoon water
2 spring onions	

Peel and finely dice the onion. Melt butter on High power (100%) for about 30 seconds. Add onion and curry powder and cook on High for 2 minutes. Trim pork and cut into thin slices. Add to onion and butter, cover and cook on High for 3 minutes. Finely slice spring onions. Reserve some for garnish and add remainder to pork with chutney and cream. Cook at 50% power for 4 minutes. Mix cornflour with water, stir into curry and cook again at 50% power for 1 to 2 minutes. Sprinkle with reserved spring onion before serving.
Serves 3 to 4.

• FRANKFURTERS IN BARBEQUE SAUCE

2 tablespoons butter	2 tablespoons tomato concentrate
1 small onion	2 tablespoons DYC vinegar
1 teaspoon dry mustard	2 tablespoons brown sugar
1 teaspoon *Fielders* cornflour	1 tablespoon Worcestershire sauce
½ cup water	450 g frankfurters

Melt butter on High power (100%) for 30 seconds. Peel and chop the onion, add to butter and cook on High for 3 minutes. Mix together mustard, cornflour and water until well blended then stir into onion and butter with tomato concentrate, vinegar, brown sugar and Worcestershire sauce. Cook on High for 2 minutes. Stir well. Place frankfurters in a flat dish, pour over sauce and cover with microwave-safe plastic wrap. Heat on 50% power for about 10 minutes or until frankfurters are heated through.
Serves 4.

• HAMBURGERS

1 small onion
2 pork sausages
400 g minced rump steak
½ teaspoon salt
Pepper
1 tablespoon DYC soy sauce

Microwave meat browning powder
8 hamburger buns
Sliced tomatoes, shredded lettuce,
   grated carrot, grated cheese,
   beetroot, cucumber, sliced
   gherkins, pickles etc

Peel and finely chop the onion. Remove skin from the sausages. Mix together onion, sausagemeat, minced steak, salt, pepper and soy sauce. Form into eight or more rounds, flattening between wet hands. Sprinkle liberally with browning powder. Cook three at a time on a flat plate on High power (100%) for about 3 to 4 minutes, turning meat halfway through cooking, so that inner edges are to the outside. This may not be necessary in some microwaves. Split buns in half or in thirds and toast cut surfaces. Serve meat onto base of buns and top with filling ingredients as wished.
Serves 6-8.

• LAMB AND MUSHROOM CASSEROLE

750 g lamb shoulder chops
1 onion
5cm piece ginger
300 g mushrooms
2 tablespoons *Fielders* cornflour

¾ cup water
3 tablespoons DYC soy sauce
½ teaspoon salt
Pepper
Chopped parsley

Trim chops and cut in half. Peel and chop the onion. Peel and very finely chop ginger. Cook onion and ginger in covered container on High power (100%) for 2 minutes. Wash and halve the mushrooms. Mix cornflour and water together. Add meat, mushrooms, soy sauce, salt and pepper to cooked onion. Stir well together, make sure meat is underneath liquid. Cover and cook on High for 10 minutes. Reduce power to 30% and cook a further 30 minutes. Serve sprinkled with chopped parsley.
Serves 4.

• LAMBS FRY AND GRAVY

400 g lambs fry
Boiling water
2 tablespoons flour

½ teaspoon salt
Pepper
Clarified butter

Place lambs fry in a dish and pour over sufficient boiling water to blanch both sides. Remove lambs fry at once, slice and remove any large tubes. Coat in flour, salt and pepper. Preheat browning dish for maximum suggested time. Add clarified butter and liver slices in a single layer. Toss gently to sear all sides before cooking on High power (100%) for 1 minute. Turn and cook on High for 2 minutes. Serve with gravy.

Gravy:

2 tablespoons gravy powder
1 to 1½ cups stock or water from blanching liver

Blend together gravy powder and stock or water and cook on High power (100%) for 2 to 3 minutes, stirring once.
Serves 4.

If cooking uneven meats cover the thinner parts with foil part way through cooking to prevent further cooking.

MEAT

• LAMB KEBABS

500 g lamb leg steaks	Pinch salt
1 bay leaf	1 tablespoon olive oil
1 sprig rosemary	16 whole dried apricots
1 sprig thyme	2 tablespoons white wine

Trim meat and cut into 3cm cubes. Crumble bay leaf, finely chop rosemary and thyme, Mix together, bay leaf, rosemary, thyme, salt and olive oil. Stir in lamb cubes and marinate 1 hour. Soak apricots in white wine for about 1 hour. Thread meat and apricots onto eight wooden or bamboo skewers. Place over large flat dish and cook at 70% power for 7 minutes. Rearrange kebabs so that outer ones are in the centre and vice versa. Cook at 70% power for another 7 minutes or until meat is cooked to your liking.
Serves 4.

• LAMB AND TOMATO CASSEROLE

2 tablespoons flour	1 teaspoon clarified butter
½ teaspoon salt	2 tablespoons tomato paste
2 teaspoons paprika	1 onion
½ teaspoon dry mustard	2 large carrots
800 g neck chops	420 g can peeled tomatoes in juice

Mix together flour, salt, paprika and dry mustard and use to coat chops. Preheat a browning dish for the maximum suggested time. Add butter and chops. Seal on both sides then cook on High power (100%) for 1 minute. Turn and cook on High 1 minute then transfer to a large casserole. Spread over tomato paste. Peel the onion and cut into rings. Peel and dice the carrots. Slice the tomatoes. Add onion, carrots, tomatoes and juice to casserole. Cover closely and cook on High for 10 minutes then cook on 30% power for 50 minutes, making sure chops are well covered with vegetables throughout. Stir once during cooking.
Serves 4-6.

• LIVER PATÉ

1 small onion	2 tablespoons brandy or sherry
2 cloves garlic	¼ teaspoon salt
3 rashers bacon	Pepper
150 g lambs fry	½ teaspoon dried tarragon
½ cup cream cheese	

Peel and roughly chop onion and garlic. Remove rind and roughly chop bacon. Cook onion, garlic and bacon on High power (100%) for 3 minutes. Thinly slice lambs fry, add to onion mixture and cover with a paper towel. Cook on High for 3 to 4 minutes or until liver is no longer pink, stirring once. Add cream cheese, brandy or sherry, salt, pepper and tarragon. Blend or process to fine paste or pass through a coarse sieve. Press into a serving dish. Chill well before serving.
Serves 4.

• MARINATED LAMB LEG STEAKS

500 g lamb leg steaks
2 teaspoons olive oil

1 tablespoon DYC soy sauce
½ teaspoon brown sugar

Marinate lamb in olive oil, soy sauce and brown sugar for about 1 hour. Preheat browning dish for maximum suggested time. Immediately add lamb, seal both sides by pressing meat onto hot surface. Cook on High power (100%) for 2 minutes, turn and cook on High for 1 minute.
Serves 4.

• MEATBALLS WITH ITALIAN TOMATO SAUCE

1 onion
500 g topside mince
1 teaspoon curry powder
½ cup soft breadcrumbs
1 egg
¼ teaspoon salt
¼ teaspoon freshly ground black pepper

1 tablespoon plum or tomato sauce
1½ teaspoons DYC soy sauce
425 g can savoury tomatoes
1 tablespoon finely chopped
    fresh basil

Peel and finely chop the onion. Put the onion, mince, curry powder, breadcrumbs, egg, salt, pepper, plum and soy sauces in a bowl. Mix together. Shape into balls about the size of a walnut. Arrange the meatballs around the outside of a large round microwave dish so the meatballs are touching. Microwave on High power (100%) for 6 minutes turning the meatballs once during cooking time. Cover and leave to stand while preparing the sauce. Pour the contents of the savoury tomatoes into a glass microwave jug. Add the basil. Cover and microwave on High for 2 minutes. Serve the meatballs on spaghetti with the sauce poured over.
Serves 4.

• MEAT LOAF

2 eggs
3 spring onions
1 small green pepper
500 g minced rump steak
1 cup soft breadcrumbs

¼ cup grated parmesan cheese
½ teaspoon dried oregano
½ teaspoon salt
Pepper
2 tablespoons toasted breadcrumbs

Beat eggs. Trim and chop spring onions. Remove seeds and dice green pepper. Mix together eggs, spring onions, green pepper, minced meat, soft breadcrumbs, Parmesan cheese, oregano, salt and pepper. Sprinkle breadcrumbs on a flat surface and turn out meat mixture. Form into a short roll about 20cm long and completely cover with toasted crumbs. Elevate on meat cooking dish or microwave rack and cook at 70% power for about 18 minutes, or until juices run clear when tested with skewer. Stand 5 minutes before slicing.
Serves 4-6.

Always elevate a roast — cook in an oven bag or covered dish. When roasting vegetables cut pumpkin larger than potato and set the kumara in the centre of the dish.

MEAT

• MICRO QUICK CASSOULET

6 sausages
2 onions
3 cloves garlic
¼ teaspoon salt
2 tablespoons oil
1 ham steak
1 bay leaf
1 sprig thyme
1 sprig parsley

820 g can baked beans
420 g can whole peeled tomatoes
Pinch salt
Freshly ground black pepper
1 teaspoon prepared mustard
2 tablespoons finely chopped parsley
2 teaspoons butter
¼ cup soft breadcrumbs

Prick sausages and microwave on High power (100%) for 6 minutes. Allow to cool slightly. Cut into 3cm pieces. Peel and chop onions. Crush, peel and mash garlic to a paste with the salt. Put oil, onion and garlic in a large microwave casserole, cook on High for 2 minutes. Chop ham. Add sausages and ham to onion. Tie bay leaf, thyme and parsley together to make a bouquet garni. Add to casserole with baked beans and tomatoes. Cover and cook on High for 10 minutes. Stir twice during cooking. Season with salt and freshly ground black pepper. Stir in the mustard. In a microwave bowl combine parsley, butter and breadcrumbs. Mix well, cook on High for 2 minutes. Stir crumb mixture and sprinkle over the cassoulet just before serving.
Serves 6.

• MINCE AND POTATO RING

1 large onion
500 g topside mince
1 egg
2 teaspoons beef flavoured stock

1 teaspoon Worcestershire sauce
2 tablespoons tomato sauce
3 medium potatoes

Finely chop the onion. Combine all ingredients in a large bowl. Grate potatoes and mix well. Push mixture into a 20 cm ring mould. Microwave on High power (100%) for about 11 minutes. Stand 10 minutes before serving.

• MINCE AND SAUSAGEMEAT RING

1 onion
1 tablespoon oil
500 g topside mince
250 g sausagemeat
½ cup soft breadcrumbs
2 tablespoons tomato chutney

2 tablespoons chopped chives
17 g packet instant gravy mix
2 eggs
¼ teaspoon freshly ground black
   pepper
2 tablespoons finely chopped parsley

Peel and finely chop the onion. Place the onion and oil in a microwave jug. Microwave on High power (100%) for 2 minutes. In a large bowl combine the onion, mince, sausagemeat, breadcrumbs, chutney, chives and gravy mix. Lightly beat the eggs. Season with pepper. Pour the eggs into the meat mixture. Mix well. Pack the mixture into a 21cm microwave ring mould. Flatten the surface. Elevate the dish and cook on High for 8 to 10 minutes. Stand for 5 minutes. Turn on to a plate and sprinkle with chopped parsley.
Serves 6 to 8.

Read your oven manual to check power level descriptions.

• MOUSSAKA

2 medium eggplants
Salt
25 g butter
1 large onion
2 cloves garlic
500 g minced rump steak

2 tablespoons tomato paste
½ cup water
½ teaspoon salt
½ teaspoon microwave browning
   liquid

Remove stem from eggplants and slice flesh. Sprinkle liberally with salt and leave 30 minutes. Melt butter on High power (100%) for 30 seconds. Peel and slice onion. Peel and finely chop the garlic. Add to butter and cook on High for 3 minutes. Break up mince, add to onion and cook on High for 4 minutes, stirring halfway through cooking. Mix in tomato paste, water, salt and micro- wave browning liquid and cook on High a further 6 minutes, stirring once. Wash sliced eggplants well and pat dry with a paper towel. Cover and cook on High for 7 minutes, stirring carefully halfway through cooking. Drain. Arrange half of the eggplant in a large flat dish, cover with half of the meat. Layer remaining eggplant and meat in dish. Pour topping over eggplant and meat in dish. Sprinkle remaining parmesan cheese and paprika over sauce. Cook at 50% power for 20 minutes.
Serves 4.

TOPPING:

50 g butter
2 tablespoons flour
1¼ cups milk

¼ cup grated parmesan cheese
2 teaspoons paprika

Melt butter on High power (100%) for about 1 minute. Stir in the flour and cook on High for 45 seconds. Blend in milk and cook on High for 3 minutes, stirring every minute. Stir in half of the parmesan cheese.

• PORK CASSEROLE

3 carrots
500 g pork pieces
1 large onion

1 packet chicken soup
300 ml water

Cut carrots into chunks, chop onion, mix with pork, chicken soup and herbs in a casserole dish. Pour water over, place a saucer on top to hold pork down. Cover and microwave on High power (100%) for 5 minutes then on 30% power for about 14 minutes.

• PORK STEAKS WITH APPLE SAUCE

4 pork steaks
1 teaspoon clarified butter
1 tablespoon mild mustard
¼ teaspoon dried tarragon

¼ teaspoon ground mixed spice
¼ teaspoon salt
Pepper
¾ cup apple sauce

Preheat browning dish for maximum suggested time, Add butter and meat and seal on both sides. Cook on High power (100%) for 1 minute. Transfer to a casserole dish and spread over mustard on both sides then sprinkle over tarragon, mixed spice, salt and pepper. Spoon over apple sauce, cover and cook at 50% power for about 10 minutes or until meat is tender and just cooked.
Serves 4.

MEAT

• POT ROAST OF BEEF

2 cloves garlic
1 kg topside roast
1 teaspoon clarified butter
1 tablespoon mild mustard
4 small pickling onions
2 carrots

2 bay leaves
½ teaspoon salt
Black pepper
½ teaspoon dried tarragon
½ cup red wine

Peel garlic, score a few times. Pierce the meat in two places with a sharp knife and insert the garlic cloves. Preheat browning dish for maximum recommended time. Add butter and meat. Seal on all sides then cook on High power (100%) for 1 minute, turn and cook on High for a further minute. Peel plckling onions and halve. Peel and cut carrots into 5cm pieces. Place meat, onions, carrots, bay leaves, salt, pepper, tarragon and red wine in casserole dish. Cover tightly and cook on 30% power for 30 minutes. Turn meat over and cook at 30% power for a further 20 minutes or until tender and juices still run slightly pink when pierced with a knife. Rest 10 minutes before cutting and serving. Serves 4.

• ROAST BEEF OR VEAL

1 large clove garlic
1 kg topside or bolar roast

1 teaspoon clarified butter
Microwave meat browning powder

Peel clove of garlic, halve and score the surface. Pierce the meat in two places with sharp knife and insert pieces of garlic. Preheat a browning dish for maximum recommended time. Add clarified butter and seal all sides of the meat well. Sprinkle with browning powder. Place on a microwave rack or meat roasting dish and cook at 70% power for 10 minutes. Turn and cook at 70% power for a further 10 minutes. For other sizes of roast meat calculate 10 minutes per 500 g at 70% power level.

• ROAST LAMB

750 g leg of lamb
2 cloves garlic
1 tablespoon finely chopped parsley

2 teaspoons grated lemon rind
2 teaspoons liquid gravy browning
1 tablespoon liquid honey

Score the skin on the lamb diagonally to form a diamond pattern. Crush and peel the garlic and cut each clove into four or six if cloves are large. Place the pieces of garlic at the points of the diamonds. Mix the parsley, lemon rind, gravy browning and honey together. Brush this mixture over the skin of the lamb. Place meat on an elevated tray. Cook at 70% power allowing 11 to 12 minutes per 500 grams for medium done or 13 to 14 minutes at 70% for well done. Cover the meat with foil and leave to stand about 10 to 15 minutes.

When using the microwave for casseroles ensure all meat to be cooked is immersed in the liquid. If not, sit a plate on top to correct the problem. Use less liquid in casseroles than you would in conventional cooking.

• ROAST PORK LOIN

1 pork loin
1 onion
½ cup chopped dried apricots
1 tablespoon finely chopped parsley
1 teaspoon lemon and pepper seasoning

¾ cup soft white breadcrumbs
2 tablespoons melted butter
Freshly ground black pepper

Cut the rind from the pork leaving some fat on the meat. Peel and finely chop the onion. Mix the onion, apricots, parsley, lemon and pepper seasoning, breadcrumbs and butter together. Season with pepper. Place the apricot stuffing lengthwise down the flap part of the loin. Roll the loin to enclose the stuffing. Tie the loin to secure the stuffing. Place on a dish that has a channel around the outside to drain the cooking juices, or place on a microwave rack. Allow 12 minutes per 500 grams on 70% power. Stand for 10 minutes or half the cooking time before carving.

• SAUSAGEMEAT RISSOLES

1 small onion
½ small green pepper
4 mushrooms
1 tablespoon Worcestershire sauce
400 g sausagemeat

1 teaspoon dried mixed herbs
½ teaspoon salt
Pepper
½ cup toasted breadcrumbs

Peel and finely chop the onion. Finely chop the green pepper and mushrooms using a food processor if available. Mix in Worcestershire sauce, sausagemeat, mixed herbs, salt and pepper. Blend well. Form into 8 to 12 rissoles using wet hands. Roll in breadcrumbs. Cook half at a time on High power (100%) for 6 to 8 minutes. Serve with tomato sauce.
Serves 4.

• SCHNITZEL ROLL UPS

500 g wiener schnitzel in 4 pieces
1 cup stuffing mix
½ cup milk

1 packet oxtail soup
1½ cups water

Add milk to stuffing mix (or prepare 1 cup homemade stuffing), place a quarter on each piece of schnitzel and roll up. Brown the surface of each roll in a frying pan or browning dish, turning in the direction of rolling. In an 18-20 cm casserole dish, mix the soup with I cup water and microwave on High power (100%) for 1 minute, stir. Place schnitzel in dish, add ½ cup water to the frying pan, dissolve browning, add to meat. Cover and microwave on High until boiling, 2 minutes, then on 30% power for 14 minutes. Check schnitzel is cooked through.

Prick foods with skins such as sausages, potatoes and tomatoes. This will help stop skins bursting and prevent the food exploding in the microwave.

MEAT

• SHEPHERDS PIE

800 g potatoes	400 g cold cooked beef or lamb
¼ cup water	¾ cup beef stock
½ cup milk	2 tablespoons tomato sauce
25 g butter	1 tablespoon Worcestershire sauce
1 teaspoon salt	½ cup grated cheese
1 onion	½ teaspoon paprika
1 teaspoon butter	

Peel potatoes and cut into large chunks. Add water, cover and cook on High power (100%) for 12 to 14 minutes or until tender, stirring once. Drain potatoes and mash then beat in milk, first measure of butter and half the salt. Peel onion and chop. Add second measure of butter and cook on High for 3 minutes. Mince or finely chop the meat. Add to onion with stock, tomato sauce, Worcestershire sauce and remaining salt to make a sloppy mixture. Transfer to a straight-sided microwave dish, cover with mashed potato and sprinkle over grated cheese and paprika. Heat on High for about 5 minutes or until very hot and cheese has melted.
Serves 4.

• STUFFED MARROW

1 onion	1 teaspoon chilli sauce
2 cloves garlic	½ teaspoon salt
1 tablespoon butter	Pepper
1 carrot	1 teaspoon dried oregano
500 g minced steak	1 marrow
¼ cup tomato concentrate	½ cup grated cheese

Peel and finely chop the onion and garlic. Cook onion, garlic and butter for 3 minutes. Peel and grate carrot. Break up minced steak and add both to onion mixture. Cook on High power (100%) for 5 minutes, stirring once during cooking. Mix in tomato concentrate, chilli sauce, salt, pepper and oregano. Wash marrow and take a horizontal slice from the top, scoop out pips and some of the flesh. If necessary take a thin slice from the bottom of the marrow to stop it wobbling. Turn meat mixture into hollowed out marrow, replace top to form a lid. Stand on two layers of paper towel on turntable and cook on High for 20 minutes. Remove lid, sprinkle with cheese and cook on High for 2 minutes or until cheese has melted.
Serves 4.

Always elevate a roast — cook in an oven bag or covered dish. When roasting vegetables cut pumpkin larger than potato and set the kumara in the centre of the dish.

• SWEET AND SOUR LAMB

1 onion	1 tablespoon DYC soy sauce
½ green pepper	2 tablespoons brown sugar
500 g lamb mince	440 g can pineapple pieces in juice
3 tablespoons *Fielders* cornflour	½ cup reserved pineapple juice
2 tablespoons DYC vinegar	

Peel and slice the onion. Deseed and thinly slice the pepper. Put the onion and mince in a microwave dish. Cook on High power (100%) for 6 minutes stirring every 2 minutes to break up the mince. Drain off any fat. Combine the cornflour, vinegar, soy sauce and brown sugar. Drain the pineapple pieces reserving half a cup of juice. Put juice in with cornflour mixture. Put the green pepper and cornflour mixture into the meat, stir. Cook uncovered on High for 5 minutes. Stir, spoon the pineapple into the meat and cook on High for a further 2 minutes.
Serves 4.

• VENISON SAUSAGES WITH APPLE AND ONION

8 venison sausages	425 g can peeled tomatoes in juice
1 small onion	½ teaspoon salt
2 cooking apples	Pepper

Prick venison sausages well all over then cook on High power (100%) for 6 minutes, rearranging on dish halfway through cooking time. Slice in thick rings. Peel and finely chop onion. Cook on High for 2 minutes. Peel core and dice the apples. Slice the tomatoes. Combine together sausage rings, onion, apples, tomatoes and juice, salt and pepper. Cover and cook on 70% power for about 15 minutes, stirring halfway through cooking.
Serves 4.

• WIENER SCHNITZEL

1 egg	¼ teaspoon salt
1 teaspoon oil	Pepper

Beat egg with oil, salt and pepper. Dip meat in egg mixture then in crumbs, press crumbs well into meat. Preheat browning dish for maximum recommended time. Add a knob of clarified butter and two schnitzel. Press down well with a fish slice and cook for 30 seconds for two small schnitzel or 1 minute for two large schnitzel. Turn and cook 30 seconds to 1 minute more. Remove and keep warm, scrape off crumbs and reheat browning dish for half maximum time. Use same cooking times for remaining meat.
Serves 4.

If cooking uneven meats cover the thinner parts with foil part way through cooking to prevent further cooking.

HINTS

Use vegetables that are as fresh as possible.
Wash well, but do not soak.
Cut into pieces of a similar size.
Cook carefully to retain as much food value as possible.
Cooking times will vary according to age of vegetables, size of pieces being cooked, amount being cooked and personal preference.

MICROWAVING

Select or cut vegetable pieces to a similar size.
Place in a shallow casserole dish and cover. If no lid, cover with microwave-safe plastic film.
Stir once during cooking time.
Add salt and other seasonings at end of cooking.
After cooking leave covered while standing. Standing time is about one-third of total cooking time.
Always undercook as cooking continues while standing.

• BAKED GREENS

½ cabbage
1-2 stalks celery
1 leek
25 g butter
1 clove garlic
¼ cup water
Salt and pepper

Finely slice the cabbage, celery and leek. Melt the butter on High power (100%) for 30 seconds. Crush and peel the garlic. Place half the cabbage in lightly greased ovenproof dish. Scatter over half celery and leeks. Repeat using remaining vegetables. Combine butter and garlic. Pour over vegetables. Pour over water and season with salt and pepper. Microwave on High power for 5-7 minutes.
Serves 4-6.

• BAKED STUFFED PUMPKIN

1 carrot
1 kumara
2 tablespoons oil
1-2 teaspoons curry powder
¼ teaspoon chilli powder
1 cup peas
½ cup whole kernel corn
¼ cup sliced almonds
1 cup coconut cream
Salt and pepper
1 medium sized pepper

Dice carrot and kumara. Cook them in oil on High power (100%) for 2 minutes. Add curry powder and chilli powder. Cook for 1 minute. Add peas, corn, almonds, coconut cream and salt and pepper and cook further 2 minutes. Slice top off pumpkin and scoop out seeds. Fill with vegetable mixture and replace top. Prick skin of pumpkin in four places. Microwave on High for 18-23 minutes.
Serves 6-8.

• BROCCOLI WITH ALMONDS

500 g broccoli
2 tablespoons butter
2 tablespoons lemon juice

2 tablespoons flaked almonds
Salt and pepper

Trim broccoli and place in a microwave dish with stalks to outer edge. Add two tablespoons of water and cook on High power (100%) for 7 to 8 minutes or until just tender. Combine butter, lemon juice, almonds, salt and pepper in a small dish and cook on High for 2 minutes. Spoon over broccoli.
Serves 4-6.

• CARROT AND PARSNIP BAKE

3 carrots
2 parsnips
¼ cup orange juice

1 tablespoon honey
1 tablespoon butter
¾ teaspoon grated root ginger

Peel and trim the carrots and parsnips. Cut into 0.5cm wide strips. Place the orange juice, honey, butter and root ginger into a large microwave casserole dish. Cook on High power (100%) for 1 to 1½ minutes or until the butter has melted. Add the carrot and parsnip and mix through the juice. Cover and microwave on High for 7 to 8 minutes or until just cooked.
Serves 5-6.

• CAULIFLOWER FRITTERS

½ cup flour
½ teaspoon *Edmonds* baking powder
Salt and pepper
1 egg

About ½ cup water
1 cauliflower
Oil for deep frying

Sift flour, baking powder, salt and pepper into bowl. Mix well. Beat in egg and enough water to make a coating batter. Divide cauliflower into florets and cook on High power (100%) for 4 to 5 minutes or until just tender but crisp. Cool. Dip cauliflower into batter and deep fry until golden brown. Drain and serve immediately.
Variation: Instead of batter, dip cauliflower into beaten egg then breadcrumbs and fry.
Serves 4-8.

• COURGETTE BAKE

3-4 medium courgettes
1 small onion
2 rashers bacon
4 eggs
½ cup flour

1 teaspoon *Edmonds* baking powder
¼ cup oil
1 cup grated cheese
Salt and pepper

Grate courgettes. Peel and finely slice onion. Derind and chop bacon. Lightly beat eggs. Add remaining ingredients. Pour into lightly greased shallow baking dish. Microwave on High power (100%) for 15 minutes.
Serves 4-8.

Every microwave oven is different. Treat cooking time given in a recipe as a guide NOT an absolute rule.

COOKING FRESH VEGETABLES

T - Tablespoon — t - teaspoon — C - cup — MW - Microwave

N.B. Microwave times for 600-700 watt oven. All cooking times HIGH unless otherwise stated.

Vegetables	Preparation	Microwave	Serving Suggestions
Asparagus	Remove woody ends.	Have similar length spears. Place tips in centre. Add 2T water. Cook 500 g 5-8 mins.	• Hot with butter, lemon, cheese or Hollandaise sauce. • Cold in salad or with French Dressing.
Aubergine (Eggplant)	Slice in 1 cm slices. Do not peel.	Add 2T butter. Cook 500 g for 6-8 minutes.	• Sprinkle with grated tasty or Parmesan cheese. • With cheese or tomato sauce.
Beans — Green, Runner and Butter	Remove string if necessary. Cut into pieces, slice diagonally or leave whole.	Add 2T water. Cook 500 g 7-14 minutes.	• With butter
Beetroot	Trim stalks and wash well. Leave skins and roots on.	Pierce skin with sharp knife. Add 2T water. Turn twice during cooking. Cook 500 g for 15-20 minutes.	• Hot — Add a little butter or with a sweet and sour or orange sauce. • Cold — slice and serve with vinegar, lemon juice or French Dressing.
Broad Beans	If young and small cook whole pods. Remove beans from older pods.	Add 2T water. Cook 250 g 6-9 mins on 90% power.	• Butter, parsley or cheese sauce.
Broccoli	Trim stalks and divide heads into florets.	If stalks thick cut cross in base. Place in dish with stalks to outer edge. Add 2T water. Cook 500 g 7-10 mins.	• Lemon, cheese or Hollandaise Sauce. • Butter and Lemon Juice.

124

Brussels Sprouts	Remove damaged leaves. Cut small cross in base of sprout.	Add ¼ c water. Cook 500 g 7-10 minutes.	• Cheese sauce or a little butter.
Cabbage	Remove damaged leaves. Shred finely.	Cook half medium cabbage (shredded) 5-7 minutes.	• Add a little butter or squeeze of lemon juice.
Carrots	Young — Scrape and leave whole. Older — Peel and slice, dice, cut into strips or grate.	Add 2T water. Cook 250 g for 4-5 minutes.	• Toss in a little butter and chopped parsley. Add 2T orange juice and 1T honey. • If older mash.
Cauliflower	Cut into florets or leave whole. If whole cut a cross in base of stalk.	Florets — Add 2T water. Cook 500 g for 6-8 minutes. Whole — wrap in plastic film and cook 500 g 8-10 minutes.	• Parsley, cheese or curry sauce. • Sprinkle with grated cheese and place under grill.
Celery	Cut into 2-3 cm pieces.	Add 1T water and 1T butter. Cook 500 g 4-6 minutes.	• Parsley or cheese sauce.
Choko	Peel, cut in half, remove the seed and slice.	Add 1T water or butter, cook 250 g 3-4 minutes.	• Add butter and chopped parsley. • Cheese, lemon or curry sauce.
Courgette (Zucchini)	If small trim ends and leave whole. Cut in half lengthwise, slice, cut in strips or grate.	Add 1T butter or water. Cook 250 g 3-4 minutes.	• Sprinkle with chopped parsley, chives or grated cheese.
Kumara	As for potatoes.		
Leeks	Remove root and trim tops. Wash well and slice.	Add 2T water. Cook 500 g for 6-8 minutes.	• Cheese or parsley sauce. • Butter and a little lemon juice.
Marrow	Peel (optional), remove seeds and slice.	Add 1T water and 1T butter. Cook 250 g for 4 minutes.	• Cheese or parsley sauce.

	Preparation	Cooking	Serving
Mushrooms	Wipe with a damp cloth. Do not peel unless skin is thick or damaged. Slice. If small leave whole.	Add 1T butter. Cook 250 g 2-3 minutes.	• Sprinkle with chopped parsley, chives or a little lemon juice.
Onions	Remove outer skin. Leave whole, cut in half or slice.	Slice and add 2T water or 1T butter. Cook 500 g for 5-8 minutes.	• Cheese or parsley sauce.
Parsnips	Peel and slice or cut lengthwise. Remove core from older parsnips.	Add 2T water. Cook 500 g for 6-8 minutes.	• Mash. Add 1T sugar, 1T lemon juice. • Sprinkle with chopped parsley.
Peas	Shell peas.	Add 1T water and 1t sugar. Cook 500 g 4-6 minutes.	• Add a little butter.
Potatoes	New — Wash and scrape. Old — Peel or scrub and leave skins on.	Boil — add ½ cup water and cook 500 g for 8-10 minutes. Bake — Prick the skin. Turn once during cooking and allow 3-4 minutes per potato.	• If old mash with a little milk, butter and pepper.
Pumpkin (Buttercup and Butternut)	Cut into wedges. Remove seeds. If roasting leave skin on, otherwise may be removed.	Add 2T water and cook 500 g for 5-6 minutes.	• Mash with a little butter and pepper.
Silverbeet	Shred leaves and cut stalks into slices.	Add 2T water. Cook 250 g for 3-4 minutes.	• Chop or purée.
Spinach	Wash well.	Place in covered pan and cook 5-8 minutes in water that clings from washing. Drain well. Do not add extra water. Cook 250 g for 2-3 minutes.	• Chop or purée. • Add pinch nutmeg and 1T cream.

Vegetable	Preparation	Cooking	Serving
Swedes	Peel and cut into slices.	Add 2T water. Cook 250 g for 5-6 minutes.	• Mash with butter and pepper.
Sweetcorn		Leave husks intact. Place cobs directly on glass tray and allow 3-4 minutes for one cob.	• Serve with butter and pepper.
Tomatoes	Cut in half.	Cook 250 g for 2 minutes.	• Sprinkle with chopped chives, basil or parsley.
Turnips	Peel and slice. If small leave whole.	Add 4T water. Cook 500 g for 6-8 minutes.	• Parsley sauce.
Yams	Wash and scrub.	Add 2T water. Cook 250 g for 5-6 minutes.	• Serve with orange sauce.

VEGETABLES

• CURRIED VEGETABLES

1 onion, sliced
2 potatoes, diced
50 g butter
2-3 teaspoons curry powder
1 tablespoon lemon juice
1 tablespoon flour
Salt and pepper

½ cup water
3-4 cups of mixture of chopped or
sliced raw vegetables such as
carrots, beans, green pepper,
courgettes, mushrooms, celery,
broccoli and cauliflower.

Peel and slice onion. Peel and dice potatoes. Place butter in large dish and microwave on High power (100%) for 30 seconds. Add onion and potato and microwave 1 minute. Add curry powder, lemon juice, flour, salt and pepper and microwave 1 minute. Add water and remaining vegetables. Cover and microwave still at High power for 6 minutes. Stir after 3 minutes.
Serves 4.

• FENNEL AND CHEESE BAKE

3 fennel bulbs
3 tablespoons lemon juice
Salt
Freshly ground black pepper

¼ cup water
2 tablespoons finely chopped parsley
¾ cup grated cheese

Wash and trim the fennel bulbs. Cut crosswise into 0.5cm slices. Place the fennel slices in a shallow microwave dish. Sprinkle with lemon juice, salt and pepper. Add the water. Cover with microwave-safe plastic wrap and microwave on High power (100%) for 7 to 8 minutes or until the fennel is tender. Drain the liquid. Sprinkle with parsley and cheese. Grill under a hot grill until the cheese is golden.
Serves 4.

• GINGER BEANS

200 g green beans
150 g butter beans
1 tablespoon butter
¼ cup finely sliced crystallised ginger

1 tablespoon poppy seeds
Freshly ground black pepper

Top and tail the beans. Cut into even-sized lengths. Place the beans, butter and ginger in a microwave dish. Cover and cook on High power (100%) for 3 minutes. Stand 2 minutes. Sprinkle with poppy seeds and season with pepper.
Serves 4.

• GLAZED VEGETABLES

1 onion, sliced
2 white turnips, thinly sliced
2 carrots, thinly sliced
3 courgettes, thinly sliced
2 tablespoons water

2 tablespoons butter
2 teaspoons brown sugar
Salt and pepper
2 tablespoons chopped parsley

Peel the onion, slice the onion, turnips, carrots and courgettes. Place water, butter, sugar, salt and pepper in pan. Microwave onion, turnip and carrot on High power (100%) for 2 minutes. Add courgette and microwave at 100% for 1 minute.
Serve sprinkled with parsley.
Serves 4.

• GREEK VEGETABLE CASSEROLE

2 onions
4-5 courgettes
4 medium potatoes
2 green peppers
2 cloves garlic

2 cups chopped tomatoes
Salt and pepper
2 tablespoons chopped parsley
¼ cup oil

Peel and slice the onion. Slice the courgettes, potatoes and pepper. Crush and peel the garlic. Place third of onion in large casserole dish. Cover with one third of courgettes, potatoes, green pepper and tomato. Sprinkle with a little garlic, salt and pepper. Repeat layers two more times until all vegetables are used. Sprinkle with parsley and oil. Cover and microwave on High power (100%) for 23-28 minutes.
Serves 6-8.

• HONEY GLAZED CARROTS AND PARSNIPS

2 to 3 medium carrots
1 to 2 medium parsnips
2 tablespoons honey

1 tablespoon lemon juice
1 tablespoon butter
2 teaspoons toasted seasame seeds

Peel carrots and parsnips and slice diagonally. Cook on High power (100%) for 4 to 6 minutes or until tender, drain. Add honey, lemon juice and butter. Shake so mixture coats carrots and parsnips. Serve sprinkled with toasted sesame seeds.
Serves 4-6.

• HOT BUTTERED BEETROOT

2-3 medium beetroot
2 tablespoons butter

Salt and pepper
2-3 tablespoons lemon juice

Peel and grate the beetroot. Place butter in dish. Microwave on High power (100%) for 30 seconds. Add beetroot and microwave 4 minutes. Add salt, pepper and lemon juice. Taste and add more pepper and lemon juice if required.
Serves 4-6.

• HOT ITALIAN MUSHROOM SALAD

300 g button mushrooms
3 tablespoons butter
2 cloves garlic
1 cup tomato purée

1 tablespoon lemon juice
1 tablespoon oil
Salt
Freshly ground black pepper

Wash and slice mushrooms. Place butter in browning dish and heat on High power (100%) for 1 minute. Add mushrooms and heat on High for 3 minutes. Crush, peel and chop garlic. Add to mushrooms with tomato purée, lemon juice, oil, salt and freshly ground black pepper. Cook on High for 1 minute.
Serves 6.

Cooking times will depend on the material of the cooking vessel. If you deviate from that specified in a recipe, the cooking time will probably differ.

VEGETABLES

• INDIAN HASSELBACK POTATOES

4 even-sized potatoes
25 g butter
2 teaspoons curry powder

¼ teaspoon grated lemon rind
1 teaspoon lemon juice

Wash potatoes. Make thin cuts crosswise almost cutting through the potato. Melt the butter on High power (100%) for 30 seconds. Stir the curry powder, lemon rind and juice into the melted butter. Spoon this mixture over the potatoes. Have cut side uppermost. Microwave uncovered on High for 10 to 12 minutes or until tender.
Serves 4.

• ITALIAN GREEN BEANS

500 g green beans
1 clove garlic
2 tablespoons oil

2 to 3 tomatoes
Salt and pepper

Slice beans on the diagonal. Place in a microwave dish with a little water and cook on High power (100%) for about 7 to 8 minutes or until tender but crisp, drain. Crush and peel garlic. Peel and chop tomatoes. Combine garlic, tomatoes, oil, salt and pepper and cook on High for 2 to 3 minutes.
Serves 4-6.

• JOHNNY APPLESEED PEPPERS

1 green pepper
1 red pepper
1 onion
2 cloves garlic

25 g butter
2 apples
Freshly ground black pepper

Core and deseed the peppers, slice finely. Peel and slice the onion. Crush, peel and mash the garlic to a paste. Put the butter into a microwave dish. Cook on High power (100%) for 1 minute or until melted. Add the onion and garlic, cover and cook a further minute on High. Add the peppers, cover and cook on High for 2 minutes. Do not peel apple, core and cut into thin slices. Add to the peppers with the ground pepper. Cover and cook on High for a further minute.
Serves 4.

• KUMARAS IN ORANGE SAUCE

500 g kumaras

1 ¼ cups Orange Sauce

Peel kumara and cut into small pieces. Cook covered with a little water on High power (100%) for 6 to 7 minutes or until just cooked. Drain and cut into 5mm slices. Arrange kumara in a microwave dish and pour sauce over. Microwave on High for 20 to 30 seconds or until hot.
Serves 4-6.

• ORANGE AND GINGER CARROTS

4-6 medium carrots
½ teaspoon ground ginger
2 tablespoons orange juice

½ teaspoon salt
2 tablespoons brown sugar
2 tablespoons butter

Peel carrots and cut into sticks. Place carrots, ginger and orange juice in dish. Microwave on High power (100%) for 5-7 minutes. Add salt, brown sugar and butter. Microwave at High for 1 minute.
Serves 4-6.

• ORANGE CRUMBED VEGETABLES

2 carrots
3 courgettes
2 stalks celery

½ cup orange juice
¼ cup frozen peas

TOPPING:

1 tablespoon butter
½ cup soft breadcrumbs
2 teaspoons grated orange rind

¾ cup grated tasty cheese
1 teaspoon chicken stock powder

Peel and slice the carrots. Slice the courgettes and celery. Place the carrots in a microwave dish. Cover and cook on High power (100%) for 5 minutes. Add the courgettes, celery, orange juice and peas. Cover and cook on High for 3½ minutes. Sprinkle topping over the vegetables. Cook uncovered for 2 minutes. Serves 4

TOPPING:

In a glass microwave jug, melt the butter on High power (100%) for 1 minute. Add the breadcrumbs, brown on High for 3½ minutes. Add the orange rind, cheese and stock powder. Mix to combine.

• POTATOES ALMONDINE

500 g even-sized potatoes
2 tablespoons water
25 g butter

Salt
Freshly ground black pepper
½ cup toasted sliced almonds

Wash the potatoes and prick skins with a fork. Place with the water in a microwave dish. Cover and cook on High power (100%) for 10 to 12 minutes or until tender. Drain the potatoes, remove the skins. Mash the potatoes, add the butter, salt and pepper to taste. Allow mixture to cool then refrigerate until cold. Divide mixture into eight and roll into cylindrical shapes using a little flour if necessary to prevent potatoes from sticking. Roll in almonds. Place on microwave dish and reheat on High for 3 minutes or until heated through. Serves 4.

• POTATO AND BACON SAVOURY

4 even-sized potatoes
1 onion
2 rashers bacon
25 g butter

½ teaspoon salt
¼ teaspoon freshly ground black
  pepper
¼ cup sour cream

Wash the potatoes and prick well with a fork. Place each potato on a paper towel. Place potatoes on a microwave rack. Microwave on High power (100%) for about 9 minutes. Leave to stand 5 minutes. While potatoes are standing, peel and slice the onion. Derind and chop the bacon. Put the butter, bacon and onion in a microwave dish. Cover and cook on High for 2 minutes. Cut the potatoes into 5mm slices. Place in a microwave serving dish. Season with salt and pepper. Spoon onion and bacon on top of potatoes. Dot sour cream on top. Return to microwave and cook on High for 50 seconds to just soften sour cream.
Serves 4.

The denser the texture of a food the longer the cooking process carries on after food is taken from the oven.

VEGETABLES

• POTATO BAKED RADISHES

4 medium potatoes
3 large radishes
25 g butter

Salt
Freshly ground black pepper

Peel and wash the potatoes. Dry with a paper towel. Cut into 1cm cubes. Trim, wash and dry the radishes. Cut into match-stick strips. Place the potatoes and radishes in a microwave dish. Add the butter and season with salt and pepper. Cover and microwave on High power (100%) for 8 to 10 minutes until the potatoes are tender. Stand 3 minutes.
Serves 4.

• POTATO CASSEROLE

3 potatoes
1 onion
1 tablespoon butter
¼ cup flour
¾ cup water

¼ cup milk
1 clove garlic
½ teaspoon salt
Freshly ground black pepper
¾ cup grated cheese

Wash and scrub the potatoes. Cut into thin slices. Peel and finely chop the onion. Combine the onion and potatoes in a microwave casserole dish. Dot with butter. In a small jug, combine the flour, water and milk. Crush, peel and mash the garlic to a paste. Add to the flour mixture. Season with salt and pepper. Stir until smooth. Pour over the potato mixture. Cover and microwave on High power (100%) for 8 minutes, stirring twice during cooking. Sprinkle the top with cheese. Microwave uncovered on High for 2 minutes. Stand 5 minutes.
Serves 4.

• POTATO WEDGE

4 potatoes
1 onion
½ green pepper
25 g butter

1 teaspoon chicken stock powder
1 tablespoon finely chopped parsley
½ cup grated cheese

Scrub potatoes then grate. Do not peel. Rinse grated potatoes under cold water, drain thoroughly. Peel and finely chop the onion. Deseed and finely chop the pepper. Melt the butter in the microwave on 50% power for 30 seconds or until melted. Add chicken stock powder, parsley, potatoes, onion and green pepper. Mix to combine. Press the potato mixture into a microwave ring pan. Sprinkle with grated cheese. Cover and cook on High power (100%) for about 10 minutes or until potato is tender. Stand 2 minutes. Serve, cut into wedges.
Serves 4.

Prick foods with skins such as sausages, potatoes and tomatoes. This will help stop skins bursting and prevent the food exploding in the microwave.

• RED AND GREEN CABBAGE CASSEROLE

¼ red cabbage
3 tablespoons red wine
¼ cup raisins
25 g butter

¼ green cabbage
2 tablespoons water
Salt
Freshly ground black pepper

Wash and remove hard core from red cabbage. Finely shred cabbage and place in a microwave casserole dish. Pour in the red wine and add the raisins and half the butter. Prepare the green cabbage in the same way. Place the cabbage in another microwave dish with the water and remaining butter. Cover and microwave both dishes together on High power (100%) for 8 to 10 minutes. Stand for 3 minutes. Combine the cabbages before serving. Season with salt and pepper.
Serves 4.

• ROSY POTATOES

4 potatoes
1 clove garlic
1 onion

1 stalk celery
25 g butter
1 teaspoon paprika

Peel the potatoes and cut into 2 cm cubes. Crush, peel and mash the garlic. Peel and finely chop the onion. Slice the celery. In a glass microwave dish melt the butter on 50% power for 30 seconds. Add the garlic, onion, celery and paprika. Toss to coat in butter. Microwave on High power (100%) for 2 minutes. Add the potatoes, toss to coat. Cover and microwave on High for 10 minutes or until potato is almost tender. Stand 2 minutes.
Serves 4.

• SCALLOPED POTATOES AND PEPPER

500 g potatoes
3 spring onions
½ green pepper

2 teaspoons butter
¼ cup sour cream

Peel and thinly slice potatoes and place in a shallow microwave dish. Cover and cook on High power (100%) for 10 minutes. Drain, set aside. Chop the spring onions, deseed and thinly slice the green pepper. Place in a microwave bowl and add the butter. Cover and cook on High for 30 seconds. Spoon the onion and pepper on top of the potato. Spread on top of the vegetables. Cook on High for about 2 minutes or until heated through.
Serves 4.

• SCALLOPINI SPECIAL

2 rashers bacon
3 to 4 scallopini
1 tablespoon butter

2 spring onions
Freshly ground black pepper

Derind the bacon. Place bacon rashers between paper towels and put into the microwave. Cook on High power (100%) for 1 ½ minutes. Stand 30 seconds. Chop into small pieces. Wash and wipe scallopini. Cut vertically into 0.5m pieces. Place in a microwave dish and dot with butter. Cover and microwave on High for 7 minutes or until cooked. Trim and finely chop the spring onions. Sprinkle the bacon pieces and spring onion over the scallopini. Season with pepper.
Serves 4.

VEGETABLES

• SHREDDED GARLIC COURGETTES

500 g courgettes
1 clove garlic

25 g butter
Freshly ground black pepper

Top and tail courgettes and grate. Crush and peel garlic. Chop finely. Place courgettes and garlic in a microwave bowl. Add butter and freshly ground pepper. Cover with microwave-safe plastic wrap. Microwave on High power (100%) for 4 minutes. Stir before serving.
Serves 4.

• SILVERBEET IN COCONUT CREAM

1 onion
Medium size bunch silverbeet

Salt and pepper
2 tablespoons coconut cream

Peel and finely slice the onion. Wash silverbeet and shred finely. Microwave silverbeet and onion on High power (100%) for 3-4 minutes (do not add water). Drain thoroughly. Season with salt and pepper. Add coconut cream and serve.
Serves 4-6.

• SPICED VEGETABLES

200 g butternut
1 potato
½ kumara
1 leek
50 g butter
½ teaspoon chilli powder

½ teaspoon cumin
1 teaspoon tumeric
½ cup chicken stock
1 courgette
Small head broccoli

Peel and deseed butternut. Peel potato and kumara. Cut vegetables into 2cm cubes. Finely slice leek. Place butter in a large microwave dish. Heat on High power (100%) for 30 seconds. Add chilli powder, cumin and tumeric. Add vegetables and toss well. Pour chicken stock over. Cover and microwave on 70% power for 15 minutes. Slice courgette and break broccoli into florets. Add to vegetables and microwave on High for 1 minute.
Serves 3.

• STUFFED BAKED POTATOES

4 medium even sized potatoes
2 tablespoons oil
½ cup milk
2 tablespoons butter

Salt and pepper
2 tablespoons chopped parsley
½ cup grated cheese
½ teaspoon paprika

Scrub potatoes and prick the skin. Brush with oil. Cook on High power (100%) for 12 to 16 minutes or until potatoes are soft. Cut lengthwise slice from top of potatoes. Scoop out potato without breaking skins. Mash potato, milk, butter, salt, pepper and parsley. Spoon mixture into potato skins. Sprinkle with cheese and paprika.
Serves 4.

For foods that have thick and thin ends such as some fish, broccoli and chicken pieces, place the thickest part to the outside of the dish.

• STUFFED CHEESY TOMATOES

2 spring onions
6 medium-large tomatoes
½ cup soft breadcrumbs
1 cup grated tasty cheese

1 tablespoon chopped fresh basil
    or 1 teaspoon dried basil
Salt and pepper

Finely slice the spring onions. Cut top off tomatoes. Scoop out pulp. Remove core and reserve rest of pulp. Combine tomato pulp, spring onions, breadcrumbs, cheese, basil, salt and pepper. Spoon filling into tomatoes. Microwave on High power (100%) for 2-3 minutes.
Serves 6.

• SWEDE BAKE

1 onion
1 small swede
¼ cup sour cream
2 tablespoons chopped parsley

Salt
Freshly ground black pepper
½ cup grated cheese

Peel the onion. Trim and peel the swede. Slice the swede and onion in a food processor. In a microwave 20cm pie dish arrange a layer of swede and a layer of onion. Spread half the sour cream over the onion. Sprinkle with one tablespoon of parsley. Season lightly with salt and pepper. Repeat the layers ending in a swede layer. Sprinkle with grated cheese. Cover and microwave on High power (100%) for 8 minutes. Stand for 5 minutes.
Serves 4.

• SWEET AND SOUR RED CABBAGE

½ red cabbage
2 apples
2 tablespoons butter

¼ cup DYC white vinegar
3 tablespoons brown sugar
Salt and pepper

Shred the cabbage. Peel and grate the apples. Microwave butter on High power (100%) for 30 seconds. Add cabbage and apple and microwave at 100% for 3 minutes. Stir. Add remaining ingredients and microwave at 100% for 11-14 minutes.
Serve hot or cold. Serves 4-6.

• SWEET AND SOUR VEGETABLES

1 large onion
1 chicken stock cube
1 tablespoon oil or butter
½ teaspoon ginger
1 tablespoon cornflour
2 tablespoons DYC soy sauce

250 g tin pineapple pieces
¼ cup DYC vinegar
4 cups mixed diced vegetables, eg.
    carrots, broccoli, green peppers,
    cabbage, cauliflower, celery,
    bean sprouts.

Peel and slice the onion. Crumble the chicken stock cube. Mix oil, onion, stock cube, ginger, cornflour, soy sauce, pineapple juice and vinegar. Microwave on High power (100%) for 2 minutes. Stir, add vegetables, cover and microwave on High until tender (5-6 minutes) stirring after 3 minutes. Stir in pineapple.

• SWEETCORN WITH MUSTARD BUTTER

4 fresh sweetcorn cobs

MUSTARD BUTTER:

50 g butter
1 teaspoon wholeseed mustard

Trim stalks from corn. Leave husks on. Cook in microwave on High power (100%) for 12 minutes. Remove husks and serve corn cobs with slices of mustard butter.
Serves 4.

MUSTARD BUTTER:

Soften the butter in the microwave on High power (100%) for 12 seconds, or until soft enough to work with. Mix in the mustard. Using a piece of grease-proof paper or plastic wrap, shape the butter into a tube. Refrigerate until firm. Slice thinly to serve.

• TASTY POTATO AND CARROT LAYER

4 potatoes
1 onion
3 carrots
½ cup hot chicken stock

1 tablespoon butter
1 tablespoon chopped parsley

Peel and thinly slice the potatoes and onion. Peel and coarsely grate the carrots. In a microwave dish place a single layer of potato then a layer of carrot. Top with a layer of onion slices. Repeat until all vegetables are used finishing with a layer of potato. Add chicken stock, dot with the butter. Cover and microwave on High power (100%) for about 15 minutes or until vegetables are tender. Sprinkle with chopped parsley.
Serves 4.

• VEGETABLE PIE

4-5 cups partially cooked vegetables. Use any combination of asparagus, broccoli, carrots, cauliflower, celery, kumara, leeks, potato, sweetcorn.
1 onion
50 g butter

3 tablespoons flour
1½ cups milk
Salt and pepper
1 cup grated cheese
200 g flaky pastry
2 tablespoons milk

Peel and slice onion. Melt butter on High power (100%) for 45 seconds. Add onion and microwave on High for 1 minute. Stir in flour, salt and pepper. Stir in milk. Microwave on High for 1 minute, stir. Repeat cooking and stirring twice more or until sauce is thick. Stir in cheese. Pour sauce over vegetables. Roll out pastry and cover pie dish. Decorate top with pastry trimmings and brush with milk. Bake at 200 degrees C for 25 to 30 minutes or until golden brown.
Serves 4-6.

Always choose a time option that undercooks the food cooked in the microwave. It is simple to add time to complete cooking.

• APPLE SAUCE

3-4 large cooking apples
1 tablespoon water
1 tablespoon butter

1 tablespoon sugar
2 cloves or few drops of lemon juice

Peel and core apples, cut into quarters. Place apples, water, butter, sugar and cloves or lemon juice in container and microwave on High power (100%) for 8 minutes or until cooked. Blend or heat with a fork until smooth.
Serve with hot or cold roast pork.
Makes about 1½ cups.

• BARBECUE SAUCE

1 onion
1 tablespoon oil
1 tablespoon flour
2 tablespoons brown sugar
2 tablespoons DYC malt vinegar

2 tablespoons tomato purée
1 teaspoon Worcestershire sauce
½ teaspoon DYC soy sauce
¾ cup water
Freshly ground pepper

Peel and finely chop the onion. Place the onion and oil in a glass microwave jug. Microwave on High power (100%) for 3 minutes. Stir in the flour, sugar, vinegar, tomato purée, Worcestershire sauce, soy sauce and water. Season with pepper. Microwave on High for 5 minutes. Stir and serve as a meat accompaniment.
Makes 1 cup.

• BRANDY OR RUM SAUCE

2 tablespoons cornflour
1 cup milk
2 tablespoons sugar

1 tablespoon butter
2 tablespoons brandy or rum
Pinch of nutmeg

Mix cornflour and a little cold milk. Combine remaining milk and sugar. Microwave milk and sugar on High power (100%) for 2 minutes. Pour over cornflour mixture. Microwave on High power for 1 minute and stir. Repeat 2 more times or until sauce is thick. Add butter, brandy or rum and nutmeg.
Serve with steamed puddings and cake type desserts.
Makes 1¼ cups.

• BUTTERSCOTCH SAUCE

1 cup brown sugar
25 g butter

½ cup cream
¾ teaspoon vanilla essence

Place the brown sugar, butter and cream in a large microwave bowl. Cover and cook on High power (100%) for 2-2½ minutes, stirring once during cooking. Add the vanilla and stir well.
Makes 1 cup.

NOTE: The sauce gets very hot, leave at least 2 to 3 minutes before serving.

If food is cooking unevenly, give a quarter turn during cooking.

SAUCES

• CHOCOLATE SAUCE

1 tablespoon *Edmonds* custard powder
1 tablespoon cocoa
1 cup milk
1-2 tablespoons sugar
1 tablespoon butter

Combine custard powder, cocoa and a little cold milk. Mix well until smooth. Combine remaining milk, sugar and butter. Microwave milk mixture on High power (100%) for 2 minutes. Add custard powder mixture. Microwave on High power for 1 minute and stir. Repeat 2 more times or until sauce is thick. Serve with fruit.
Makes 1 cup.

• CUMBERLAND SAUCE

2 teaspoons grated orange rind
2 teaspoons grated lemon rind
¼ cup orange juice
2 tablespoons lemon juice
2 tablespoons finely chopped onion
½ cup redcurrant jelly
2 tablespoons port
Salt and pepper

Put the rinds and juices into a microwave glass measuring jug. Add the onion. Microwave on High power (100%) for 2 minutes or until onion is cooked. Stir in the jelly and port. Season with salt and pepper to taste.
Makes about 1 cup.

• CUSTARD SAUCE

2 teaspoons *Edmonds* custard powder
1 cup milk
1 egg
1 teaspoon sugar

Combine custard powder and a little of the cold milk. Heat remaining milk on High power (100%) for 2 minutes. Pour over custard powder mixture and cook on High for 1 minute. Stir then cook for a further minute and stir. Lightly beat the egg and sugar and pour over the custard. Cook on 50% power for 1 minute, stir.
Makes 1 cup.

• FRUIT SAUCE

1 onion
1 tablespoon oil
1 green apple
1 tablespoon flour
¼ cup sultanas
½ cup chopped dates
1 tablespoon brown sugar
2 tablespoons DYC malt vinegar
½ cup water
Salt
Freshly ground black pepper

Peel and finely chop the onion. Place the onion and oil in a glass microwave jug and cook on High power (100%) for 3 minutes. Core but do not peel the apple. Cut into cubes. Stir the flour into the onion. Add the apple, sultanas, dates, sugar, vinegar and water. Season with salt and pepper. Microwave on High for 7 minutes. Serve with meat dishes.
Makes about 1¾ cups.

• HOLLANDAISE SAUCE

50 g butter
1 tablespoon lemon juice
2 egg yolks

¼ cup cream
½ teaspoon dry mustard
¼ teaspoon salt

Melt butter on High power (100%) for 30 seconds. Add lemon juice, egg yolks and cream. Microwave on High for 1 minute, stirring after 30 seconds. Add seasonings and beat until smooth.
Serve with vegetables such as asparagus and broccoli, or fish.
Makes ¾ cup.

• JAM SAUCE

4 tablespoons jam
4 tablespoons water

2 teaspoons lemon juice

Combine jam, water and lemon juice and microwave on High power (100%) for 1 minute.
Serve with steamed puddings.
Makes ½ cup.

• LEMON SAUCE

2 tablespoons *Fielders* cornflour
1 cup water, chicken stock or water
   vegetables cooked in

1 lemon
1 egg
Salt and pepper

Combine cornflour and water. Microwave on High power (100%) for 2 minutes. Grate the rind from the lemon and squeeze the juice. Lightly beat lemon rind, juice and egg. Pour hot liquid over egg mixture, beating constantly. Microwave on High for 20 seconds to heat through. Season to taste. Serve with fish, vegetables or chicken.
Makes 1¼ cups.

• MUSTARD SAUCE

1 egg
¼ cup sugar
1 tablespoon flour
1 teaspoon dry mustard

Salt and pepper
1 cup water or liquid corned beef
   cooked in
¼ cup DYC malt vinegar

Beat egg and sugar. Add flour, mustard, salt and pepper. Stir in water and vinegar gradually. Microwave on High power (100%) for 1 minute and stir. Repeat two more times or until sauce is thick.
Makes 1½ cups.

Always use microwave-safe plastic wrap for microwave cooking. This is marked on the box or wrapper.

SAUCES

• ORANGE SAUCE

1 small onion
2 tablespoons butter
¾ cup water
2 tablespoons *Fielders* cornflour

½ teaspoon chicken stock powder
2 teaspoons grated orange rind
½ cup orange juice
Salt and pepper

Peel and finely chop onion. Place butter and onion in a glass microwave jug. Cook on High power (100%) for 3 minutes or until onion is soft. Combine water and cornflour. Add with chicken stock, orange rind and juice to jug. Cook on High for 1 minute, stir then repeat cooking and stirring twice more or until sauce is thick.
Makes 1¼ cups.

• PEPPER AND CORN SAUCE

1 tablespoon butter
1 tablespoon flour
½ teaspoon finely chopped green
   peppercorns

1 cup milk
½ cup whole kernel corn
½ teaspoon sugar

Place the butter in a microwave bowl. Cover and cook on High power (100%) for 15 seconds. Stir in the flour and green peppercorns. Gradually stir in the milk. Cover and cook on 70% power for 3 minutes, stirring every minute. Add the corn and cook on 70% power for a further minute. Serve with vegetables or as a meat accompaniment.
Makes about 1½ cups.

• SPICED ORANGE SAUCE

¼ cup sugar
1 tablespoon *Fielders* cornflour
½ teaspoon cinnamon
1 cup water

2 teaspoons butter
2 tablespoons orange juice
1 teaspoon grated orange rind

Blend the sugar, cornflour and cinnamon with a little water. Add remaining water, butter, orange juice and orange rind. Microwave on High power (100%) for 1 minute and stir. Repeat 2 more times or until sauce is thick.
Serve with steamed puddings and cake type desserts.
Makes about 1½ cups.

• SWEET AND SOUR SAUCE

4 tablespoons brown sugar
2 tablespoons *Fielders* cornflour
4 tablespoons DYC white vinegar

1 tablespoon DYC soy sauce
1 cup water or liquid vegetables
   cooked in

Combine brown sugar, cornflour, vinegar, soy sauce and vegetable liquid. Microwave on High power (100%) for 1 minute and stir. Repeat two more times or until sauce is thick.
Serve with vegetables.
Makes 1¼ cups.

• WHITE SAUCE

2 tablespoons butter
2 tablespoons flour

Salt and pepper
1 cup milk

Melt butter on High power (100%) for 20 seconds. Stir in flour, salt and pepper. Stir in milk. Microwave on High power for 1 minute and stir. Repeat two more times or until sauce is thick.

Variations

Cheese Sauce	Stir in ½ cup grated tasty cheese after cooking sauce.
Curry Sauce	Add 1-2 teaspoons curry powder when adding flour.
Mock Hollandaise Sauce	Make white sauce and remove from heat. Stir in one beaten egg yolk and drop by drop 1 tablespoon lemon juice. Reheat but do no boil.
Onion Sauce	Add 1 sliced onion that has been cooked in water or butter to white sauce.
Parsley Sauce	Add 2-4 tablespoons chopped parsley to white sauce.
Tomato Sauce	Omit milk and use ½ cup tomato purée and ½ cup water.

Makes one cup.

• APPLE AND RHUBARB SPONGE

500 g rhubarb
2 apples

¼ cup orange juice
2 teaspoons grated orange rind

Wash and trim the rhubarb. Cut the rhubarb into 6cm lengths and place around the edge of a large microwave dish. Core and slice the apples and place in the centre of the rhubarb. Pour over the orange juice and sprinkle with the rind. Cover and cook on High power (100%) for 4 to 5 minutes or until tender. Transfer to a six-cup capacity glass microwave souffle dish. Spoon over the cake batter. Return to the microwave and cook on High for 4½ to 5 minutes. The cake may still be moist in the centre but will complete cooking on standing time. Stand 5 minutes before serving.
Serves 4.

Cake Batter:

2 tablespoons butter
¼ cup sugar
Few drops vanilla essence
1 egg

½ cup flour
½ teaspoon *Edmonds* baking powder
3 tablespoons milk

Cream the butter, sugar and vanilla essence. Add the egg and beat well. Sift the flour and baking powder together. Fold the sifted dry ingredients into the creamed mixture alternately with the milk.

• APPLE CUSTARD FLAN

Pastry:

1 cup flour
¼ cup wholemeal flour
3 tablespoons sugar

75 g butter
About ¼ cup cold water

Sift the flour into a bowl. Add the wholemeal flour and sugar. Rub in the butter until the mixture resembles fine crumbs. Add the water, mixing to form a stiff dough. Turn the dough on to a lightly floured board. Knead lightly. Roll out the pastry and use it to line a 20cm microwave flan dish. Prick the base several times with a fork. Chill the base for 15 minutes. Elevate and microwave on High power (100%) for 4 to 4½ minutes, or until the pastry looks dry. Fill the pastry case with the filling. Elevate the dish and microwave on High for 5 to 6 minutes or until set. Cover the flan with a paper towel and stand for 5 minutes. Serve cold.
Serves 6.

Filling:

3 medium apples
1 cup milk
¼ cup sour cream
2 tablespoons sugar

2 tablespoons Fielders cornflour
2 egg yolks
1 teaspoon grated lemon rind
Cinnamon

Peel, core and thinly slice the apples. Arrange the apple slices over the pastry base. In a large glass microwave jug, combine the milk, sour cream, sugar and cornflour. Beat the mixture until the cornflour is well mixed. Microwave the mixture on High for 3 to 4 minutes. Stir then add the egg yolks and lemon rind. Beat well. Pour the custard over the apples. Sprinkle the top with cinnamon.

• APPLE SORBET

½ cup castor sugar
1½ cups hot water
4 granny smith apples

½ cup lemon juice
¼ cup dry white wine
2 egg whites

In a glass microwave jug combine the sugar and water. Microwave on High power (100%) for 2 minutes, stir, continue cooking for a further 2 minutes or until sugar has dissolved. Allow to cool. Peel, core and roughly chop the apples. Place in the bowl of a food processor with the lemon juice. Process to a smooth purée. Combine apple purée and cool syrup. Pour into a suitable freezer container. Freeze until slushy, stirring occasionally to mix the outside edges into the centre. Transfer mixture to a mixing bowl, beat thoroughly. Add the wine. Beat egg whites until stiff but not dry. Fold egg whites into apple mixture. Refreeze until firm. To serve spoon sorbet into chilled glasses.

• BAKED APPLES

4 granny smith apples
2 tablespoons liquid honey

½ teaspoon mixed spice
¼ cup chopped walnuts

Wash the apples. Cut a slice from the top of each apple. Core each apple. If necessary level the apple from the bottom so they stand upright. Place apples in a microwave dish. Replace the lids. Add about one tablespoon of water to the dish. Cover with microwave-safe plastic wrap. Microwave on 30% power for 10 minutes or until apple feels soft. Remove from microwave. Scoop the flesh out leaving the skins intact. Mix the pulp, honey, mixed spice and walnuts together. Spoon back into the skins. Replace lids. Serve with a little whipped cream.
Serves 4.

• BANANA CARAMEL CRUMBLE

3 to 4 medium firm bananas
2 tablespoons butter

¼ cup brown sugar
2 tablespoons cream

Peel bananas and cut in half then slice lengthwise. Put butter in a microwave pie plate. Cover and microwave on High power (100%) for 30 seconds or until melted. Add the sugar and cream, stir to combine. Microwave on High for 1½ to 2 minutes or until slightly thickened. Add the bananas turning each to completely coat with the sauce. Microwave on High for 30 seconds. Transfer to a serving plate then sprinkle with topping.

TOPPING:

½ cup *Flemings* rolled oats
¼ cup flour
½ teaspoon *Edmonds* baking powder

50 g butter
½ cup fancy sliced almonds

Put the rolled oats, flour and baking powder into a food processor. Pulse to combine. Add butter, process until crumb-like. Spoon crumble onto a flat plate. Microwave on High power (100%) for 3 minutes or until crisp. Shake the plate from time to time during cooking. Stir in the almonds.

Warm brandy in the microwave before igniting for flambé dishes.

DESSERTS

• BANANA CUSTARD

¼ cup sugar
¼ cup Edmonds custard powder
2 cups milk
1 tablespoon butter

1 tablespoon cream
3 to 4 bananas
About 1 tablespoon lemon juice
Whipped cream for garnish

In a glass two-litre microwave measuring jug combine sugar and custard powder. Gradually add the milk, stirring all the time. Microwave on High power (100%) for about 6 minutes, stirring every 2 minutes or until custard boils and thickens. Stir in the butter and cream, continue stirring until butter has melted. Peel bananas and slice into four individual serving dishes. Spoon lemon juice on top. Pour custard evenly over bananas. Cool, then refrigerate until cold. Serve garnished with whipped cream.
Serves 4.

• BANANA ISLANDS

2 tablespoons butter
2 ripe bananas
¼ cup brown sugar
¼ cup milk

½ cup flour
½ cup wholemeal flour
½ cup wheatgerm
1 teaspoon *Edmonds* baking powder

CARAMEL SAUCE:

2 tablespoons butter
1 cup brown sugar

1 cup boiling water

Mix the butter, bananas, brown sugar and milk together. Place the flour, wholemeal flour, wheatgerm and baking powder in a bowl. Add the banana mixture and mix lightly. Drop tablespoon lots into the caramel sauce. Cover and cook on High power (100%) for about 6 minutes or until risen and set. Stand for 4 minutes.
Serves 6.

CARAMEL SAUCE:

Place the butter, sugar and boiling water in a shallow microwave dish. Cook on High power (100%) for about 4 minutes, or until thickened. Stir well.

• BREAD AND BUTTER PUDDING

25 g butter
2 teaspoons grated lemon rind
2 raisin and egg rolls
½ cup milk

½ cup cream
½ cup brown sugar
1 egg
Lemon slices to garnish

In a glass two-litre microwave measuring jug put the butter. Cover and microwave on 50% power for about 40 seconds or until melted. Add the lemon rind. Break the bread rolls into small pieces, add to the butter mixture. Stir to coat. Add the milk, cream and sugar. Leave to stand 15 minutes. Separate the egg. Mix egg yolk into bread mixture. Beat egg white until stiff but not dry. Carefully fold into bread mixture. Spoon into four round half-cup capacity microwave dishes. Elevate and microwave on 50% power for 8 to 10 minutes or until set. Stand 1 minute then unmould onto serving plates. Garnish with lemon slice if wished.
Serves 4.

Chocolate melted in the microwave holds its shape until mixed.

• CARAMELISED ORANGES

½ cup sugar
½ cup water
¼ cup boiling water

Julienne orange rind
4 oranges

Put the sugar and first measure of water in a glass microwave measuring jug, stir. Microwave on High power (100%) for about 2 minutes, stir until all the sugar has dissolved. Return to the microwave and continue cooking for about 6 minutes or until sugar starts to caramelise. The moment the mixture starts to caramelise remove from the microwave as cooking will continue. Leave until golden in colour. With care pour the second measure of water into the caramel, stir to combine. Serve poured over the oranges and garnish with julienne of orange rind.
Serves 4.

TO PREPARE ORANGES:

Remove all skin and pith from the oranges. Using a few pieces of rind cut into very thin strips. Pour boiling water over rind and leave to stand until ready to use. The oranges can be left whole or segmented by cutting in between the membranes with a small sharp knife and carefully easing the segments out. If leaving the oranges whole you can make cuts in between the membranes but leave the fruit whole. This will make for easier eating.

• CARROT PUDDINGS WITH LEMON SAUCE

50 g butter
1 cup grated carrot
½ cup brown sugar
2 tablespoons oil
1 egg

¾ cup flour
½ teaspoon baking soda
½ teaspoon *Edmonds* baking powder
1 ½ teaspoons mixed spice
1 teaspoon cinnamon

In a two-litre microwave jug melt the butter on High power (100%) for 60 seconds. Stir in the grated carrot, sugar, oil and egg, mix to combine. Sift the flour, baking soda, baking powder, mixed spice and cinnamon together. Fold the sifted ingredients into the carrot mixture. Mix until all the ingredients are moistened. Spoon mixture into four individual microwave dishes. Elevate and microwave on 70% power for about 5 minutes or until just set. Leave to stand 2 minutes. Serve with Lemon Sauce.
Serves 4.

• LEMON SAUCE

25 g butter
2 tablespoons sugar
2 teaspoons grated lemon rind
1 ½ tablespoons *Fielders* cornflour

½ cup lemon juice
¼ cup water
1 tablespoon citrus marmalade

Put the butter in a glass microwave measuring jug. Cover and microwave on High power (100%) for about 40 seconds or until melted Combine sugar, lemon rind and cornflour. Gradually stir in the lemon juice, mixing to a smooth paste. Add the water. Transfer to the jug containing the butter. Microwave on High for about 3 minutes or until mixture boils and thickens. Stir occasionally during cooking time. Add the marmalade. Serve with Carrot Puddings.

Warm citrus fruits in the microwave to extract more juice.

• CHOCOLATE SPONGE PUDDING WITH ALMOND CUSTARD

125 g softened butter
½ cup sugar
2 eggs
1 cup flour
1 teaspoon *Edmonds* baking powder

¼ cup cocoa
½ cup milk
1 cup *Edmonds* custard
½ teaspoon almond essence

Cream butter and sugar until light and fluffy and sugar has dissolved. Do not over-beat. Beat in eggs one at a time, beating well after each addition. Sift flour, baking powder and cocoa together. Fold into creamed mixture. Fold in the milk, mixing well. Lightly grease a one-litre glass microwave measuring jug. Pour batter into jug. Cover loosely with a paper towel. Microwave on High power (100%) for 6 minutes, or until pudding is just set. Leave to stand 5 minutes. Unmould onto a serving dish. Serve with *Edmonds* custard flavoured with half a teaspoon of almond essence.
Serves 4 to 5.

• CHOCOLATE SPONGY PUD

75 g butter
1 teaspoon vanilla essence
½ cup brown sugar
1 egg
¾ cup flour

1 teaspoon *Edmonds* baking powder
2 tablespoons cocoa
¼ teaspoon baking soda
¼ cup sour cream
1 tablespoon oil

Cream butter, vanilla and sugar together. Add the egg, beating well. Sift flour, baking powder, cocoa and baking soda together. Fold the dry ingredients into the creamed mixture, then fold in the sour cream and oil. Divide batter evenly among four microwave china teacups or microwave pudding bowls. Elevate and microwave on 50% power for 5 minutes or until just cooked. Stand for 2 minutes. Serve with *Edmonds* custard.
Serves 4.

• CREAMY CHEESE PIE

250 g packet gingernut biscuits
50 g butter

Place gingernuts in a food processor and pulse to form fine crumbs. Melt butter and pour into biscuit crumbs. Mix well. Press into a 24cm diameter microwave pie plate. Cook on High power (100%) for 1 to 2 minutes.

FILLING:

2 eggs
250 g pot cream cheese
½ cup sugar

1 teaspoon almond essence
250 g pot sour cream
½ teaspoon cinnamon

Beat eggs, cream cheese, sugar, almond essence, sour cream and cinnamon in a mixing bowl. Beat until smooth. Place in microwave and cook on 30% power for 10 minutes, stirring every 2 minutes. Pour into baked crumb crust. Cook on 30% power for a further 3 minutes, or until set. Chill several hours before serving.
Serves 6 to 8.

• CREME CARAMELS

½ cup sugar
3 tablespoons boiling water
2 cups milk

4 eggs
¼ cup sugar

Place the first measure of sugar and boiling water in a microwave dish. Cook on High power (100%) for 5 to 6 minutes or until the caramel begins to brown. Pour one-sixth into six, half-cup capacity microwave ramekin dishes. Heat the milk on High for 2 minutes. Beat the eggs and sugar to combine and stir into the milk. Mix well. Pour one-sixth through a sieve into each ramekin dish. Cook on 70% power for 6 to 8 minutes or until the custard sets. Stir once during cooking and halfway through cooking, rearrange ramekins to avoid uneven cooking. Refrigerate for 2 to 3 hours. Turn out just before serving.
Serves 6.

NOTE: If your microwave cooks unevenly, it is advisable to cook these for a reduced time, one at a time.

• CHRISTMAS PUDDING

1 cup raisins
1 cup sultanas
½ cup brandy
1 apple
½ cup brown sugar
2 teaspoons cinnamon
1 teaspoon allspice

¾ teaspoon ground cloves
1 teaspoon grated orange rind
3 eggs
¼ cup flour
100 g butter
2 cups flaked rice

Soak the raisins and sultanas in the brandy for 1 hour. Peel, core and grate the apple. Add to the soaked fruit. Add the brown sugar, cinnamon, allspice, cloves and orange rind. In a small bowl lightly beat the eggs with the flour. Melt the butter and add to the egg mixture. Pour over the fruit. Add the flaked rice and stir well to combine. Stand for 10 minutes. Press the mixture into a greased and floured seven-cup capacity microwave mixing bowl. Smooth the surface. Cover with microwave-safe plastic wrap. Pierce a hole for ventilation. Elevate and microwave on 50% power for 15 to 16 minutes. Stand covered for 5 to 7 minutes.
Serves 10 to 12.

• CRUMBLE

¾ cup wholemeal flour
¾ cup rolled oats
¾ cup brown sugar

1 teaspoon cinnamon
1 teaspoon ginger
75 g butter

Mix dry ingredients and rub in butter. Cover the bottom of a pie or casserole dish with stewed fruit eg. apples, pears, rhubarb, spread crumble mixture on top and microwave on High power (100%) for 7-8 minutes.

Use the microwave to soften cream cheese, butter and ice-cream for easier use in some recipes.

DESERTS

• CUSTARD FLAN

1¼ cups flour
¼ teaspoon *Edmonds* baking powder
75 g butter

1 egg yolk
Chilled water
Fresh fruit to decorate

CUSTARD FILLING:

2 tablespoons *Edmonds* custard powder
2 egg yolks
2 tablespoons sugar

1½ cups milk
Few drops vanilla or lemon essence

Sift the flour and baking powder into a bowl. Cut in the butter until it resembles fine crumbs. Add the egg yolk and sufficient chilled water to form a dry dough. Roll pastry out and use it to line a 20cm microwave flan dish. Prick the base and sides all over. Chill for 30 minutes. Cook on High power (100%) for 5 to 6 minutes or until the pastry in the centre of the dish is cooked. Pour in the custard filling and cover. Chill until set. Cover with fresh fruit before serving. Serves 6.

CUSTARD FILLING:

In a glass microwave jug, blend the custard powder, egg yolks and sugar. Stir in the milk. Cook on High power (100%) for 3 to 4 minutes, stirring frequently. Flavour with vanilla or lemon essence.

• DATEY PEARS

½ cup chopped dates
3 tablespoons finely chopped walnuts
1 tablespoon brown sugar

¼ teaspoon mixed spice
4 pears

SAUCE:

½ cup chopped dates
1 tablespoon butter
¼ cup water

¼ teaspoon mixed spice
¼ cup cream or top milk

Mix the dates, walnuts, brown sugar and mixed spice together. Core the pears and fill each pear with one-quarter of the date and walnut mixture. Cover and cook on High power (100%) for 8 minutes. Stand for 5 minutes. Add the cooking juice from the pears to the sauce. Serve hot with the sauce. Serves 4.

SAUCE:

Mix the dates, butter, water and spice together. Cook on High power (100%) for 1 minute. Beat together until smooth. Stir in the cream or top milk.

To test a jam for setting drop a teaspoon of jam on to a cold saucer. Leave to cool for a few minutes. If the jam surface wrinkles when lightly touched the jam is ready.

• FRUIT TRIFLE

1 ½ tablespoons *Edmonds* custard
powder
1 tablespoon sugar
1 cup milk
2 cups cake crumbs

300 ml cream
½ cup fruit pulp such as strawberry,
peach or passionfruit
1 tablespoon icing sugar
1 tablespoon fruit pulp for garnish

Combine custard powder and sugar in a large glass microwave jug. Gradually add the milk, mixing until smooth. Microwave on High power (100%) for 4 minutes, stirring after 2 minutes. Add the cake crumbs to the custard. Spoon custard mixture into six coupé dishes. Refrigerate until firm. Whip the cream until thick. Add the first measure of fruit pulp and icing sugar to the cream. Spoon fruit pulp mixture on top of custard smoothing the top surface over. Refrigerate for about 30 minutes. Before serving spoon a little of the second measure of fruit pulp over each dish for garnish.
Serves 6.

• GINGER PUDDING

100 g butter
½ cup brown sugar
1 egg
2 tablespoons lime marmalade
1 cup flour

2 teaspoons ground ginger
1 teaspoon *Edmonds* baking powder
½ teaspoon baking soda
2 tablespoons warm milk

Cream butter and sugar together until light and fluffy. Add the egg and marmalade beating well. Sift the flour, ginger and baking powder together. Fold into the creamed mixture. Dissolve the baking soda in the milk and add to the batter. Spoon evenly among six individual microwave pudding dishes. Elevate and microwave on 50% power for 4 to 5 minutes or until just set. Stand for 2 minutes.
Serves 6.

• HOT SPICED FRUIT SALAD

About 1 cup figlets (small figs)
8 prunes
4 dried mango slices
8 dried apricots
¼ cup white wine
¼ teaspoon ground ginger

¼ teaspoon mixed spice
2 tablespoons brown sugar
½ cup orange juice
227 g can pineapple rings
Coconut flakes or shreds for garnish

Put the figs, prunes, mango slices and apricots into a glass one-litre microwave measuring jug. Add the wine, ginger, mixed spice, sugar and orange juice. Cover and microwave on High power (100%) for 8 minutes. Leave to stand about 5 minutes or until the fruit is plump. Drain the pineapple rings and cut each ring into three. Add to the hot fruit salad. Serve in individual serving dishes garnished with coconut flakes or shreds.
Serves 4.

Only use plastics designed for microwave use. Many plastics contain impurities and cannot be used safely in the microwave.

DESSERTS

• KIWIFRUIT AND ORANGE SHORTCAKE

1¼ cups wholemeal flour	1 egg
1 teaspoon *Edmonds* baking powder	3 kiwifruit
¼ cup brown sugar	¼ teaspoon grated orange rind
¼ teaspoon almond essence	2 oranges
50 g butter	1 cup cream

Place the wholemeal flour, baking powder and brown sugar in a bowl. Add the almond essence. Rub in the butter until the mixture resembles fine crumbs. Lightly beat the egg. Add to the flour mixture. Knead together to form a soft dough. Divide the dough in half and roll out to form two l5cm diameter circles. Place one circle on a microwave plate lined with greaseproof paper. Cook on High power (l00%) for l½ to 2 minutes or until the edge is firm and the surface is dry. Stand for 2 minutes. Cut into six wedges. Repeat with the second circle but do not cut. Cool. Peel the kiwifruit and cut into rings. Grate quarter of a teaspoon of orange rind from one orange. Using a small sharp knife peel the oranges removing the white pith. Cut into segments by cutting between the membrane. Whip the cream and fold in the orange rind. Use the uncut circle as the base. Pile on the prepared fruit and cream. Top with wedges of the second circle.
Serves 6.

• LEMON CHEESECAKE

BASE:

75 g butter	1 cup gingernut biscuit crumbs

Put the butter into a glass one-litre measuring jug. Microwave on High power (100%) for about 1½ minutes or until melted. Add biscuit crumbs, mixing well. Line a 22cm flan dish with microwave-safe plastic wrap. Press biscuit crumb mixture into prepared dish. Microwave on High for 1 minute. Pour the filling over the base, smoothing over the top surface. Elevate and microwave on 50% power for about 12 minutes, or until cheesecake is almost set in the centre. Cool then refrigerate until firm. When firm spread with a thin layer of lemon honey.
Serves 6 to 8.

FILLING:

2 x 250 g pots firm cream cheese	¼ cup milk
¾ cup sugar	2 teaspoons grated lemon rind
¼ teaspoon salt	¼ cup lemon juice
2 tablespoons flour	4 eggs

Remove foil covers from the cream cheese. Microwave on High power (100%) for 1 minute, or until softened. In a glass microwave bowl beat the cream cheese with a wooden spoon until creamy. Add the sugar, salt and flour. Gradually beat in the milk, lemon rind and juice. Add the eggs one at a time, beating well after each addition. Microwave on High for about 8 minutes or until heated, stirring every 2 minutes. Use to fill base.

TOPPING:

About ½ cup lemon honey

A watchful eye while microwave cooking is crucial.

• LEMON SELF SAUCING PUDDING

PUDDING:

125 g butter
½ cup sugar
2 eggs
1 teaspoon grated lemon rind

¾ cup flour
1½ teaspoons *Edmonds* baking powder
About ¼ cup milk

SAUCE:

1 teaspoon grated lemon rind
¼ cup castor sugar
1 tablespoon *Fielders* cornflour

1½ cups boiling water
½ cup lemon juice

PUDDING:

Cream butter and sugar until light and fluffy. Add the eggs one at a time beating well after each addition. Stir in the lemon rind. Sift flour and baking powder together. Fold flour into creamed mixture. Add sufficient milk to make a thin batter. Spoon batter into a lightly greased glass casserole dish. Sprinkle cornflour mixture on top then carefully spoon the boiling water mixture over the pudding. Microwave on High power (100%) for 10 minutes or until pudding is just cooked. Serve dusted with icing sugar if wished.
Serves 6.

SAUCE:

Combine lemon rind, sugar and cornflour. Mix boiling water and lemon juice together.

NOTE: If boiling water is not spooned gently over pudding then an uneven surface will result.

• MICROWAVE APRICOT SPONGE

425 g can apricot halves
50 g butter
¼ cup sugar
1 egg
½ cup flour

½ teaspoon *Edmonds* baking powder
¾ teaspoon cinnamon
½ teaspoon ground allspice
¼ cup milk
Icing sugar

Drain the apricots. Arrange apricot halves on the bottom of two small 13cm diameter microwave dishes. Microwave on High power (100%) for 3 to 4 minutes or until the fruit is hot. Cream the butter and sugar. Add the egg beating well. Sift the flour, baking powder, cinnamon and allspice. Fold into the creamed mixture. Stir in the milk. Pour batter over the hot fruit dividing the batter equally between the two dishes. Cover with a paper towel. Microwave on High for 3 to 3½ minutes or until the surface is sponge-like. Dust with icing sugar. Serve hot.
Serves 4.

Cooking times will depend on the material of the cooking vessel. If you deviate from that specified in a recipe, the cooking time will probably differ.

DESSERTS

• ORANGE SULTANA PUDDINGS

75 g butter
½ cup brown sugar
2 teaspoons grated orange rind
2 eggs
1 cup cake crumbs

1 cup flour
1 teaspoon *Edmonds* baking powder
½ cup sultanas
½ cup orange juice

Put the butter in a glass microwave measuring jug. Cover and microwave on High power (100%) for 1½ minutes or until melted. Stir in the sugar and orange rind. Lightly beat the eggs. Add to the butter mixture with the cake crumbs, stir to combine. Sift flour and baking powder together. Fold flour and sultanas into orange mixture alternately with the orange juice. Pour batter into four lightly greased teacups. Elevate and microwave on 70% power for about 5 minutes or until just set. Serve with *Edmonds* custard.
Serves 4.

• OVERNIGHT PUDDING

1½ cups cake crumbs
¾ cup wholemeal flour
1 teaspoon *Edmonds* baking powder
2 teaspoons mixed spice
¼ teaspoon salt
¼ cup *Flemings* oat bran

½ cup brown sugar
1 teaspoon grated lemon rind
½ cup shredded suet
¾ cup mixed fruit
1½ cups hot milk

Put the cake crumbs into a mixing bowl. Sift flour, baking powder, mixed spice and salt into the crumbs. Add the oat bran, sugar and lemon rind. Stir to combine. Stir in the suet and mixed fruit. Pour in the milk, mix to combine. Transfer to a four-cup capacity microwave pudding basin. Leave to stand overnight. Next day cover, elevate and microwave on High power (100%) for about 20 minutes or until skewer comes out clean when inserted. Serve hot with *Edmonds* custard.
Serves 6 to 8.

• PEAR CRISP

½ cup flour
½ teaspoon *Edmonds* baking powder
¼ teaspoon salt
¼ cup Flemings rolled oats
¼ cup coconut

50 g butter
¼ cup brown sugar
2 tablespoons chocolate chips
820 g can pear halves

Sift flour, baking powder and salt together. Add rolled oats and coconut. Cut through the butter until crumb-like. Stir in the sugar and chocolate chips. Drain the pears. Place the pears flat side down in a microwave dish. Sprinkle crumble mixture on top. Microwave on High power (100%) for about 6 minutes, or until crumble is cooked. Serve with cream or *Edmonds* custard.
Serves 6.

• PUMPKIN PIE

BASE:

75 g butter
1 cup biscuit crumbs
¼ cup *Flemings* oat bran

2 tablespoons brown sugar
Whipped cream
Chopped walnuts

FILLING:

1 cup cold mashed pumpkin
½ cup brown sugar
¾ cup cream
½ teaspoon mixed spice

¼ teaspoon ground nutmeg
¼ teaspoon cinnamon
3 eggs

In a glass microwave one-litre measuring jug put the butter. Cover and microwave on High power (100%) for 1 minute or until melted. Stir in the biscuit crumbs, oat bran and sugar, mix to combine. Line a 22cm microwave flan dish with microwave-safe plastic wrap. Press biscuit mixture onto the wrap. Microwave on High for 1 minute. Set aside. Pour filling onto crumb crust. Elevate and microwave on 70% power for about 15 minutes or until filling is just set. Cool. Refrigerate until firm. Serve garnished with whipped cream and walnuts.

FILLING:

In a food processor put the pumpkin, sugar, cream, mixed spice, nutmeg, cinnamon and eggs. Process until smooth. Transfer filling to a glass microwave jug. Microwave on 70% power for about 5 minutes or until warmed through, stirring occasionally.

• QUICK PEACH MERINGUE

820 g can peach slices
¼ teaspoon mixed spice

Drain the peach slices and arrange on the base of a glass microwave pie plate. Sprinkle with mixed spice. Spoon meringue on top of peaches. Microwave on High power (100%) for about 4 minutes or until meringue is set.
Serves 4 to 5.

MERINGUE:

3 egg whites
¾ cup castor sugar

½ teaspoon vanilla essence
½ teaspoon DYC white vinegar

Beat egg whites until stiff but not dry. Gradually add the castor sugar beating constantly. Beat in the vanilla and vinegar.

• RICE PUDDING

¾ cup rice
1 tablespoon *Edmonds* custard
3 tablespoons brown sugar

1 cup boiling water
600 ml milk

Mix dry ingredients in a bowl, add half the milk and the water. Cover and microwave on High power (100%) until boiling, about 4 minutes. Stir adding the remaining milk. Microwave on 30% power until thick and creamy, about 27 minutes, stirring after 10 minutes and 20 minutes.

DESERTS

• ROCKY CHOCOLATE MOULD

100 g dark chocolate	250 g packet wine biscuits
100 g butter	1 tablespoon crystallised ginger
1 egg	1 tablespoon glacé cherries
2 tablespoons brown sugar	1 tablespoon grated orange rind

Place the chocolate and butter in a bowl. Melt on High power (100%) for about 2 minutes, stirring once. Beat the egg and brown sugar until well blended. Gradually add the melted chocolate mixture. Break the biscuits into rough pieces. Chop the ginger and cherries roughly. Add the biscuit pieces, ginger, cherries and orange rind. Press the mixture into 5 lightly oiled dariole moulds. Refrigerate for 3 hours. To serve, dip the moulds quickly in hot water and invert onto serving dish. Serve with whipped cream.
Serves 5.

• SAVARIN

1½ teaspoons DYC dried yeast	1/8 teaspoon salt
1 teaspoon sugar	75 g butter
¼ cup tepid milk	2 eggs
1½ cups flour	1 teaspoon sugar

Combine yeast and first measure of sugar. Sprinkle yeast mixture on top of the tepid milk. Leave in a warm place until frothy. Sift flour and salt into a mixing bowl. Put the butter in a glass microwave jug. Cover and microwave on High power (100%) for about 1½ minutes or until melted. Lightly beat the eggs. Pour the yeast mixture onto the flour. Add the butter, eggs and second measure of sugar. Beat well with hands for about 15 minutes or until smooth and forms a ball. Dough should be of a soft consistency. Lightly grease a 20cm microwave ring mould. Place dough in mould. Microwave on 30% power for 1 minute. Leave to stand 10 minutes. Repeat until dough has doubled in bulk. Elevate and microwave on High for 3 minutes or until just set. Leave to stand 5 minutes. Spoon syrup over Savarin while hot. Unmould to serve. Serve warm.
Serves 8-10.

RUM SYRUP:

1 cup sugar	3 tablespoons dark rum
¾ cup hot water	½ cup lemon juice

Put the sugar and water into a glass microwave jug. Microwave on High power (100%) for 3 minutes or until sugar has dissolved. Stir occasionally during cooking time. Add the rum and lemon juice.

• STEAMED PUDDING

125 g butter	1 teaspoon mixed spice
¾ cup brown sugar	1 teaspoon baking soda
1 cup milk	1¼ cups wholemeal flour
1½ cups mixed fruit	

Place butter, sugar, milk and fruit in a 17cm bowl and microwave on High power (100%) for 5 minutes. Add spice and soda stirring well. Mix in flour, cover with plastic wrap and microwave on High for 5-6 minutes. Invert onto a serving plate.

• STRAWBERRY SPONGE FLAN

1 cup flour
¼ cup *Fielders* cornflour
2 teaspoons *Edmonds* baking powder
¼ teaspoon salt
¾ cup castor sugar
2 egg yolks

5 tablespoons oil
5 tablespoons water
2 egg whites
8 large strawberries for decoration
Whipped cream

FILLING:

1 ½ cups strawberries
250 g pot cream cheese

2 tablespoons icing sugar
1 cup whipped cream

Sift the flour, cornflour, baking powder and salt together. Add the castor sugar. Beat the egg yolks, oil and water together. Stir the egg mixture into dry ingredients. Mix until moistened. Beat egg whites until stiff. Gently fold the egg whites into the batter. Pour into a 20cm microwave sponge flan dish. Cook on High power (100%) for 5 to 6 minutes, or until just set. Allow to stand for 5 minutes before turning on to a cooling tray. When cold, spoon the filling into the centre. Halve the strawberries and arrange decoratively on top of the filling. Garnish with whipped cream if wished.
Serves 6 to 8.

FILLING:

Wash and hull the strawberries, purée in a food processor. Beat cream cheese until soft, beat in the icing sugar. Fold in the whipped cream and strawberry purée. Use this to fill the sponge.

To test a jam for setting drop a teaspoon of jam on to a cold saucer. Leave to cool for a few minutes. If the jam surface wrinkles when lightly touched the jam is ready.

• BOTTLED PEARS

2 cups sugar
4 cups water

8 medium pears

Heat the sugar and water in a large saucepan. Stir to dissolve the sugar. Peel, core and cut the pears into quarters. Have two litre preserving jars hot. Pack the fruit into the jars. Cover with the hot syrup leaving a 2cm gap at the top. Cover the jars with microwave-safe plastic wrap. Pierce two to three times. Microwave the two jars on High power (100%) for 10 to 12 minutes. Watch for small bubbles rising from the bottom. This indicates the fruit has cooked. Overflow with the remaining boiling syrup. Cover with a seal and screw band, making sure the rim of the jar is clean and dry. The jar has an airtight seal when the seal is concave. Makes 2 x 1 litre jars.

• BLACKBERRY JAM

600 g blackberries
¼ cup water

2 teaspoons lemon juice
2½ cups sugar

Wash the blackberries. Put into a large microwave bowl. Add water and lemon juice. Cook on High power (100%) for 5 minutes. Stir in the sugar. Cook on High for 15 minutes, stirring mixture after 3 minutes to help dissolve sugar, then again after another 3 minutes. Cook until the jam gives a setting test. Pour into hot sterilised jars. Cover and label.
Makes about 2 cups.

• GRAPE JELLY

1 kg ripe outdoor black grapes
3 tablespoons lemon juice

¾ cup water
Sugar

Wash grapes, remove stalks. Place fruit, lemon juice and water into a large microwave bowl. Cook on High power (100%) for 25 minutes. Stir every 5 minutes. Strain through a jelly bag. Measure the juice. Return to the microwave bowl. Cook in the microwave on High for about 6 minutes or until the mixture boils. Remove from oven and add three-quarters of a cup of sugar for each one cup of juice. Stir until sugar has dissolved. Cook on High for about 25 minutes or until jelly sets when tested on a saucer. Stir every 5 minutes during cooking. Pour into clean, hot, dry jars. Cover and label when cool.
Makes about 2 cups.

• GREEN TOMATO CHUTNEY

700 g green tomatoes
2 apples
1 onion
2 cloves garlic

¾ cup DYC vinegar
¾ cup sugar
1 teaspoon salt

Wash and roughly chop the tomatoes. Peel and core the apples. Peel the onion and garlic. Roughly chop the apple, onion and garlic. Put the tomatoes, apple and onion in a large microwave dish. Add the vinegar, sugar and salt. Stir. Cover and cook on High power (100%) for about 10 minutes. Uncover and cook on High for 10 minutes or until mixture is thick. Stir occasionally. Place in hot sterilised jars. Seal when cold. Makes about 3 cups.

DESSERTS Hot Fruit Salad, Carrot Pudding with Lemon Sauce and ►
Caramelised Oranges.

• LEMON HONEY

3 eggs
1 cup sugar
50 g butter

1 teaspoon grated lemon rind
½ cup lemon juice

Place the eggs and sugar in a two-litre glass microwave jug. Beat until well mixed. Add the butter, lemon rind and juice. Microwave on High power (100%) for 8 minutes, stirring with a whisk every 2 minutes. Cool for a few minutes then pour into hot dry jars. Seal when cold.
Makes 2 cups.

• MARROW AND GINGER JAM

1 kg marrow
½ cup lemon juice

1 teaspoon grated root ginger
3 cups sugar

Peel marrow and cut in half horizontally. Scoop out the seeds. Cut the flesh into 1 cm cubes. Place into a large microwave casserole dish. Add the lemon juice and ginger. Cover with microwave-safe plastic wrap and leave overnight. Next day microwave the marrow uncovered on High power (100%) for 10 minutes. Stir in the sugar and microwave on High for a further 15 to 18 minutes or until the jam mixture gives a setting test. Pour jam into hot sterilised jars and seal.
Makes 3 x 350ml jars.

• STRAWBERRY JAM

500 g strawberries
1 teaspoon grated lemon rind

¼ cup lemon juice
2 cups sugar

Wash and hull the strawberries. Place in a large microwave bowl. Add the lemon rind and juice. Cook on High power (100%) for 4 minutes or until strawberries are soft. Add the sugar, stir. Cook on High for 20 minutes or until jam gives a setting test. Stir the jam occasionally during cooking. Stand for 5 minutes before pouring into hot sterilised jars.
Makes about 2 cups.

• TROPICAL PEACH FRUIT BUTTER

1 tablespoon lemon juice
¾ cup peeled, diced peaches
2 eggs

1 cup sugar
½ cup passionfruit pulp
100 g butter

Pour the lemon juice over the peaches and toss lightly to coat. Beat the eggs and sugar together in a microwave dish. Add the diced peaches and passionfruit pulp. Stir to combine. Cut the butter into small pieces, add to the dish. Cover and cook on High power (100%) for about 6 minutes. Do not allow mixture to boil. Stir occasionally. Mixture should be thick enough to coat the back of a wooden spoon. Allow to cool slightly before pouring into hot dry sterilised jars.
Makes 2 cups.

◄ JAMS AND SWEETS Green Tomato Chutney, Strawberry Jam, Lemon Honey, After Dinner Truffles, Coconut Ice and Rocky Road.

• AFTER DINNER TRUFFLES

½ cup raisins
¼ cup finely chopped crystallised
  ginger
2 tablespoons dark rum
1 teaspoon grated lemon rind
2 cups stale cake crumbs

¼ cup Flemings oat bran
¼ cup sugar
25 g butter
100 g cooking chocolate
About ½ cup coconut

Chop the raisins. Put the raisins, ginger, rum and lemon rind into a bowl. Leave for 15 minutes. Add cake crumbs, oat bran and sugar. Put the butter and chocolate into a glass microwave measuring jug. Microwave on High power (100%) for 1 minute, stirring after 30 seconds. Pour the melted ingredients into the fruit mixture, mixing well. Roll into balls about the size of a walnut. Roll in coconut. Refrigerate until firm. Serve with coffee.
Makes about 25.

• BRAZIL NUT TOFFEE

1 cup sugar
¼ cup liquid glucose
¼ cup water

1 cup roasted brazil nuts
50 g butter
¼ teaspoon vanilla essence

Grease or foil line a 20cm shallow square tin. Put the sugar, glucose and water into a two-litre glass microwave measuring jug. Stir to combine. Microwave on High power (100%) for 5 minutes, or until sugar has dissolved, stir after every 2 minutes. Continue microwaving for 6 minutes until hard crack stage on a sugar microwave thermometer. Remove toffee from microwave using oven gloves. Roughly chop the nuts. Quickly stir in the butter, nuts and vanilla. Pour into prepared tin. Mark into squares. Leave until cold and set. Carefully lift the toffee from the tin then break into pieces. Store in an airtight container.

NOTE: To roast nuts — coat nuts in about 1 teaspoon oil. Microwave in a shallow glass plate or dish. Microwave on High for about 5 minutes, shaking the plate occasionally.

• CHOCOLATE FUDGE

200 g packet cooking chocolate
400 g can sweetened condensed milk
50 g butter

2 teaspoons grated orange rind
½ cup coconut

Lightly grease or foil line a 15cm shallow cake tin. In a two-litre glass microwave measuring jug put the chocolate, sweetened condensed milk and butter. Microwave on 70% power for 5 minutes, stirring after 2 minutes. Stir again then microwave on 70% for about 10 minutes, or until thick and dark. Beat in the orange rind and coconut. Pour into prepared tin, smoothing the top surface. Refrigerate for about 24 hours or until firm. Cut into small squares.

Always use microwave-safe plastic wrap for microwave cooking. This is marked on the box or wrapper.

• CHOC RUM SQUARES

375 g cooking chocolate
½ cup Flemings oat bran
Pinch salt
400 g can sweetened condensed milk

1 tablespoon rum
½ cup chopped walnuts

Break chocolate into small pieces. Place in a microwave mixing bowl. Microwave on High power (100%) for about 2 minutes or until melted when stirred. Add the oat bran and salt. Stir to mix. Return to the microwave for about 30 seconds. Stir in the condensed milk, rum and walnuts until combined. Spread mixture evenly into a foil lined 20cm square tin. Cover and refrigerate until firm. When firm turn out onto a board and cut into squares.

• COCONUT ICE

4 cups icing sugar
100 g butter
¼ cup milk

1 teaspoon vanilla essence
1½ cups coconut
Red food colouring

Put icing sugar, butter and milk into a two-litre glass microwave measuring jug. Microwave on High power (100%) for 3 to 4 minutes, until mixture has melted. Add vanilla and coconut, beat until thick. Divide in half. Add a few drops of food colouring to one portion. Press white portion into a 20cm square tin. Leave until thickened before pressing pink mixture on top. Refrigerate until firm.

• CREAMY FUDGE

150 g pot cream cheese
1½ tablespoons milk
1 teaspoon vanilla essence

2½ cups icing sugar
200 g packet cooking chocolate
½ cup chopped walnuts

Put cream cheese into a microwave bowl. Microwave on High power (100%) for 25 seconds or until softened. Beat in milk, vanilla and icing sugar until smooth. Break the chocolate into a bowl. Microwave on High, stirring after every 30 seconds until just melted. Fold chocolate and nuts into cream cheese mixture. Spread into a non-stick foil lined 20cm square shallow cake tin. Refrigerate until set. Cut into squares.

• ROCKY ROAD

1 cup blanched peanuts
1 teaspoon oil
190 g packet pink and white
    marshmallows

75 g vegetable shortening
400 g cooking chocolate

Combine peanuts and oil in a shallow dish. Microwave on High power (100%) for about 6 minutes, stirring frequently. Allow to cool. Roughly chop the peanuts. Line a 20cm square cake tin with non-stick foil. With a pair of floured scissors cut the marshmallows in half. Put half the marshmallows and nuts onto the base of the prepared tin. Break chocolate into a bowl, add vegetable shortening. Microwave on High for about 2 minutes or until melted when stirred. Pour half the chocolate over the marshmallow and nuts. Sprinkle rest of marshmallows and nuts over chocolate. Finally top with remaining chocolate. Refrigerate until set. Cut into squares to serve.

Chocolate melted in the microwave holds its shape until mixed.

• VANILLA AND WALNUT FUDGE

50 g butter	½ teaspoon vanilla essence
1 cup sugar	2 tablespoons raisins
6 tablespoons milk	½ cup finely chopped walnuts

Foil line a 16cm x 8cm tin or dish. Put the butter in a two-litre glass microwave measuring jug. Cover. Microwave on High power (100%) for 40 seconds or until melted. Stir in the sugar and milk mixing well. Microwave on High for 6 to 8 minutes, or until soft ball stage is reached. Remove from the microwave. Stir in the vanilla. Finely chop the raisins. Add the raisins and walnuts to vanilla mixture. Beat with a wooden spoon until mixture is thicker and lighter in colour. Spread into prepared container. Using a sharp knife mark into squares. When cold cut into squares.

NOTE: A metal ice cube tray can be used or alternatively a piece of stiff cardboard can be used to make a container smaller.

INDEX

Use the microwave to soften cream cheese, butter and ice-cream for easier use in some recipes.

Always choose a time option that undercooks the food cooked in the microwave. It is simple to add time to complete cooking.

First edition, 1989
First printing 40,000 copies

© Copyright, Bluebird Foods Ltd, 1989

Recipes developed by Bluebird Foods Ltd
and Robyn Martin & Associates, Auckland.

Book production by Gordon Ell, The Bush Press
Typesetting: Jacobsons Graphic Communications

Printed by The Book Printer
in Melbourne, Australia

Published by Beckett Publishing, 1989,
P.O. Box 31-042, Milford, Auckland 9,
on behalf of Bluebird Foods Ltd, Auckland.

ISBN 0-908676-47-6

Every microwave oven is different. Treat cooking time given in a recipe as a guide NOT an absolute rule.